WHEN CHURCH HURTS

By

Colin A Mason

MAPLE
PUBLISHERS

When Church Hurts

Author: Colin A Mason

Copyright © Colin A Mason (2023)

The right of Colin A Mason to be identified as author of this work has been asserted by the author in accordance with section 77 and 78 of the Copyright, Designs and Patents Act 1988.

First Published in 2023

ISBN 978-1-915492-68-5 (Paperback)
      978-1-915492-69-2 (Hardback)
      978-1-915492-70-8 (E-Book)

Book cover design by:

    Christian Book Editor
    https://christianbookeditor.uk/

Book layout by:

    White Magic Studios
    www.whitemagicstudios.co.uk

Published by:

    Maple Publishers
    Fairbourne Drive, Atterbury,
    Milton Keynes,
    MK10 9RG, UK
    www.maplepublishers.com

CONTENTS

Acknowledgements

Words could not adequately convey my gratefulness to my heavenly Father for bringing me to a place where I could get this book completed and all the experiences that He has enabled me to come through to be where I am today.

The most significant person that has been with me throughout my journey, good and bad, bitter, and sweet, highs and lows is my wife, Yvonne. She has stood firm all the way even at times when the journey has been personally difficult for her, but her faith has not wavered and in God she continued to trust. Our marriage is certainly a match made in heaven and I could never have imagined the very special journey that we would embark on together twenty-one years ago, and God's utter faithfulness in bringing us through all the storms of life into greener pastures and an astonishingly bright future.

There has also been some significant people and organisations that have been instrumental in my educational, mentoring and healing journey namely the late Pastor Winston Folkes and his widow Pastor Brenda Folkes, Reverend Nezlin J Sterling of Institute of Theology & Christian Counselling (ITCC) including my tutors, Reverend Dr Marvin Sanguinetti, Reverend Dr Ruthlyn Bradshaw, Dr Paige-Patric Samuels and Dr R David Muir. Also, Prophet Paul Barfett (although I know he is not one for using titles), Prophets Ron and Jane Joliff from Columbus, USA, Eric McKenna of Eagle Raisers, Ellel Ministries at Pierrepont, Glyndley Manor and

Blairmore House, Mark Iles, and Kevin McStay at School for Prophecy and Liz Evans and her team at Love Has a Voice. Last and not least MACSAS (Minister and Clergy Sexual Abuse Survivors) and The Hope for Survivors in the USA. God has strategically used them in various ways to bring healing, teaching, mentoring, support, words of encouragement and razor-sharp prophetic insight over the years. Their support has given me a greater understanding of the love of God, and I am so grateful for the way that they have allowed themselves to be used by Him in our lives.

Introduction

This book is definitely not an attack on the church, but written with a desire to promote healing and reconciliation in the body of Christ. I want to reach out to many people that have been bitterly disappointed and left badly hurt by their disconcerting encounters in the context of church, church groups, or church organisations. Sadly, these troubling interactions have left many feeling that their experiences were of little importance to God. After all, why would a supposedly loving God allow such negative and often traumatic things to happen to them? Where was God when all this was happening? Why did He not step in and do something? If the church really cared about me, why did I suffer such horrendous treatment? Why were people in leadership who represent God acting in such an unkind, horrible, and abusive manner? The questions are endless, but the truth is that God never intended for His people to be misused, abused, ill-treated, belittled, rejected, and hurt in various shapes or forms within the context of His Church. He hates and doesn't want this, especially from those who were supposed to model His love and compassion and offer positive and helpful guidance.

Henceforth, why do people end up being enormously hurt in Church? Part of the reason is that there are often people in leadership positions who are themselves wounded and hurting. These people require inner healing, and quite possibly, deliverance. As the saying goes, hurt people hurt people and wounded people often inflict wounds on others. Sometimes, people are mistakenly placed in leadership positions by those who can't discern their true character, which then causes a great deal of damage within the Body of Christ. For example, an individual may be given a leadership position because they are gifted in a particular area without acknowledging that their character requires more time to develop. Then some take it upon themselves to do their own thing and gather a following of people around them who are immature and lacking in discernment. There is also the arch-enemy of God, Satan, who hates the Church passionately and will use deceived individuals in their brokenness to cause absolute havoc in churches.

Over the years, the term "spiritual abuse" has become widely used to cover the various kinds of hurt people encounter within the confines of church organisations, churches, or church groups. So, what exactly do we mean by spiritual abuse? Spiritual abuse or church hurt is the mistreatment of a person in the name of God, faith, religion, or church organisation at the expense of their spiritual well-being. It could further be described as when members of the clergy or anyone in a leadership role control, dominate, or manipulate others at the expense of their spiritual well-being. Within this context, it would be appropriate to include Sunday school teachers, House group leaders, choir directors, department heads, or anyone within a recognised leadership role. However, spiritual abuse can also go the other way: when an individual or group controls, dominates, or manipulates a person or persons in leadership positions.

For the most part, this book will focus on spiritual abuse by leaders and how they negatively impact those they are leading. The Bible has a great deal to say about leadership's treatment of those they lead. Also, it talks about God's view when people mistreat or abuse their God-given leaders, but the latter dimension will be discussed in another book.

This book seeks to address issues arising when people do not properly understand what godly leadership looks like, how those leaders are expected to behave, and their job function in proximity to the wider Body of Christ as servant leaders. Suppose a person does not have a sound biblical understanding of the role of leadership; in that case, many people can be negatively affected as we will see abusive behaviour operating amongst God's people under the guise of "strong leadership". Unfortunately, people may willingly accept negative treatment by leadership that is not scriptural because they genuinely believe that God is using their leader(s). Because of this mindset, the leaders are beyond reproach. This does not mean all wrong behaviours connote a bad leader. After all, none of us is perfect, but certain things should be a bright red warning flag to us that something is not quite right.

Often, those brave enough to highlight the wrong things can become labelled as "the problem", enabling the leadership to carry on in their role without self-reflectively examining their behaviour and being challenged. Congregants and other leaders can inadvertently collude with wrong behaviour, become part of the problem too, and be used by leadership to support an abusive system. This is often because of fear and people mistakenly feeling that they should "not be rebellious" by accepting whatever leadership is dishing out and commanding them to do. Some people have grown up in such settings, making it harder to challenge things as they are made to feel that they are backslidden or their hearts are defiant.

The expected result is that many have come to the erroneous conclusion that Church is not the place for them.

Sadly, in some instances, they also reject God as they believe their treatment and what they experienced to be synonymous with God. Nothing could be further from the truth. God loves His people, and it pains Him when leaders misrepresent Him and cause deep hurt to the flock that He loves.

Whenever bank tellers are being trained to identify fake banknotes, they are taught to identify everything about an authentic note. Their familiarity with the real thing will instantly highlight for them whenever a fake note crosses their path. Likewise, to identify a false leader, we need to be conversant with the real deal. So, the best place to start our journey is by looking into God's word and discovering the various ways we can identify authentic leaders. What should they look like? How should they behave? How should they treat the people they lead? What does God say about His preferred type of leader, etc.? Understanding biblical leadership is essential for people to avoid and escape situations that can be potentially harmful to them. The understanding of biblical leadership is also a tremendous benefit in the healing journey and recovering from church hurts. This is because when your eyes become open to God's truth, you will be set free from any erroneous beliefs about God and why you were hurt in such ways. Most importantly, you will be better placed to ensure that you regularly fellowship with believers and leaders that are safe and conducive to your personal growth and spiritual maturity.

Chapter 1

Godly Leadership –
What does it look like?

The best place to start our journey is in the word of God. After all, this is the bedrock of the Christian faith, so we need to find out whatever God has to say about leadership and what we should and should not expect to see in godly leaders. One of the earliest examples of choosing leadership can be found in the Book of Exodus, where Moses' father-in-law, Jethro, advises Moses. After recognising that Moses could potentially wear himself out dealing with the people, Jethro gave sound advice on the characteristics Moses should seek when choosing leaders to support his ministry:

> *Now listen to me; I will advise you, and may God be with you [to confirm my advice]. You shall represent the people before God. You shall bring their disputes and causes to Him. You shall teach them the decrees and laws. You shall show them the way they are to live and the work they are to do. Furthermore, you shall select from all the people competent men who [reverently] fear God, men of truth, those who hate dishonest gain; you shall place these over the people as leaders of thousands, of hundreds, of fifties and of tens. They shall*

> *judge the people at all times; have them bring*
> *every major dispute to you but let them judge*
> *every minor dispute themselves. So, it will be*
> *easier for you, and they will bear the burden*
> *with you (***Exodus 18:19-22***; AMP).*

Moses' father-in-law's advice on choosing good leaders highlighted certain areas Moses needed to consider and what he needed to do before placing anyone in a leadership position:

- They had to be taught the things of God and trained in line with their role
- They needed to have reverential fear and respect for the things of God
- They needed to have integrity and honesty
- They should not be easily bribed or swayed by personal financial benefits
- They should be given areas of responsibility that match their capability

This was extremely important because they would have an influence on other people's lives. Therefore, putting the wrong person in any role could have disastrous results and negatively affect the people. This was not a decision to be taken lightly, and Moses would have to deliberate over what he knew of these potential leaders' characters. This decision process is vital when placing anybody in the position of leadership because leadership roles will certainly expose anywhere there are flaws in a person's character. Although it is a joy working with and leading people, other people's flaws, wounds, attitudes, behaviours, and characters can be quite challenging to any leader.

Things can go seriously wrong when there is a lack of careful, prayerful consideration before placing anyone in a leadership position. One of the biggest problems I have seen regarding the area of church leaders is sometimes the person never had the level of maturity to handle their role and was not adequately trained or prepared. In other instances, people may simply be in a role because they are best friends with the leadership, have a particular gifting or talent, or possess a charismatic and vibrant personality. A common mistake often made is placing someone in the role of leader because they flow with spiritual gifts, for example, prophecy. They could be potentially elevated prematurely without their character maturing enough to match their spiritual giftedness. Spiritual giftedness is never a good reason on its own to place someone in the position of leadership. Another common mistake senior leaders make is giving someone leadership positions simply because they are a great public speaker and can preach well. Although these are good attributes to have, without good character, it will almost certainly lead to the person's downfall. These reasons alone are never good enough to place someone in a leadership role. There must be a much wider consideration given.

Let's look at two versions of the same passage in 1st Peter that give us biblical insight into Peter's guidance about what we should expect to see in godly leaders:

> Shepherd and guide and protect the flock of God among you, exercising oversight not under compulsion, but voluntarily, according to the will of God; and not [motivated] for shameful gain, but with wholehearted enthusiasm; not lording it over those assigned to your care [do not be arrogant or overbearing], but be examples [of Christian living] to the flock [set

13

a pattern of integrity for your congregation] (**1 Peter 5:2-3**; *AMP*).

Shepherd [tend] God's flock for whom you are responsible [which is under your care]. Watch over [Oversee] them because you want to, not because you are forced. That is how God wants it. Do it because you are happy [eager] to serve, not because you want money [of greed]. Do not be like a ruler over people [lord it over those; dominate those; you are responsible for [under your care; those allotted (to you) but be good examples to them [the flock]. (**1 Peter 5:2-3**; *EXB*)

The apostle Peter, who was personally discipled by the Lord Jesus Christ, gives us insight into the attitude we should expect to see in leaders.

1. It is a role they should want to do happily and willingly, not forced into.
2. Their mindset should be one of servitude. They are to serve the people; the people are not there to serve them.
3. Money should never be a motivational factor in leading people.
4. The leadership style should be loving, caring, and kind, not domineering.
5. Their behaviour and lifestyle should be a good example for others to follow.

If a leader does not have a sound biblical understanding of their role and what it entails, it might cause a great deal of hurt for those under their care. In many instances, because of this lack of understanding, some leaders believe the people they are leading are there to serve them and to build their personal empire. The way they treat those they regard as beneath them sets a terrible precedent for how believers and those leading them should behave. If a leader is abusive and bullying, people who do not clearly understand biblical leadership will erroneously believe that this is how things are supposed to be amongst God's people.

Although they may not like the treatment, they will accept it as the "will of God" and therefore suppress any misgivings they may have, which should be a red flag to them, highlighting the fact that they are in real danger. Sadly, many believers in the Body of Christ now accept things they would not ordinarily tolerate outside of a church context because they wrongly believe this is how things should be. It is as if they abandon common sense at the church doors and switch off their discernment of what is right or wrong. They let go of their own sense of self and behave almost clone-like in submitting themselves to a system detrimental to their spiritual and emotional well-being. This is why people stay in church groups damaging to their spiritual well-being and feel unable to leave, even though their gut feelings are screaming at them that something is seriously wrong.

The Apostle Paul gives very clear and detailed criteria about what we should expect to see in those leading other people in the context of the Church.

> *This is a faithful and trustworthy saying: if any man [eagerly] seeks the office of overseer (bishop, superintendent), he desires an excellent task. Now an overseer must be blameless and beyond reproach, the husband of one wife, self-controlled, sensible, respectable, hospitable,*

*able to teach, not addicted to wine, not a
bully nor quick-tempered and hot-headed, but
gentle and considerate, free from the love of
money [not greedy for wealth and its inherent
power—financially ethical]. He must manage
his own household well, keeping his children
under control with all dignity [keeping them
respectful and well-behaved] (for if a man does
not know how to manage his own household,
how will he take care of the church of God?).
and He must not be a new convert, so that
he will not [behave stupidly and] become
conceited [by appointment to this high office]
and fall into the [same] condemnation incurred
by the devil [for his arrogance and pride]. And
he must have a good reputation and be well
thought of by those outside the church, so
that he will not be discredited and fall into the
devil's trap (**1 Timothy 3:1-7**; AMP).*

Although the apostle Paul speaks specifically about
male leadership, the same standards apply to females in
leadership positions, many of which exist throughout the
Body of Christ.

Paul's list of requirements for overseers:
1. Blameless – a life beyond reproach, virtuous,
   righteous, scrupulous
2. Husband of one wife or wife of one husband –
   faithful
3. Self-controlled – able to control themselves in all
   situations and stay calm

4. Sensible – practical, no-nonsense, level-headed, reasonable, wise

5. Respectable – well-thought of, decent, upright, proper

6. Hospitable – welcoming, warm, friendly, generous, kind

7. Able to teach – able to teach godly principles and rightly divide God's Word

8. Not addicted to wine or strong drink

9. Not a bully or quick-tempered or hot-headed

10. Free from the love of money – financially ethical

11. Gentle and considerate

12. Manages his household well – children are respectful and well behaved

13. Not a new convert

14. Must have a good testimony among those who are outside the church.

Here, Paul is referring to someone who will oversee other leaders and churches in the senior role of a bishop or an elder. Their whole life should be an example to others, especially to other leaders within the Body of Christ. This does not mean that they are perfect in every way. We all fall short in some way, shape, or form. However, the role of a leader in the Body of Christ is a high calling, and with it comes great responsibility. Paul is saying here that anyone considering such a role needs to think soberly and honestly whether they truly have the capacity to engage in what can be a potentially very challenging position on many levels—emotionally, physically, and spiritually.

It is quite easy to look at a person and make all kinds of assumptions about their character based on their position or title. A leader who is excellent in a particular area may be seriously lacking in other vital areas. For example, a person may have exceptional preaching ability and rightfully divide the Word of God but have no integrity regarding money or are abusive towards congregants. On the other hand, they may also flow accurately in spiritual gifts, e.g., a prophecy, whilst secretly struggling with pornography or illicit sexual relationships.

Paul continues in 1st Timothy by highlighting characteristics that should be evident in the life of those serving as deacons:

> *Deacons likewise must be men worthy of respect [honourable, financially ethical, of good character], not double-tongued [speakers of half-truths], not addicted to wine, not greedy for dishonest gain, but upholding and fully understanding the mystery [that is, the true doctrine] of the [Christian] faith with a clear conscience [resulting from behaviour consistent with spiritual maturity]. These men must first be tested; then if they are found to be blameless and beyond reproach [in their Christian lives], let them serve as deacons* (**1 Timothy 3:8-10**; *AMP*).

A deacon is someone who serves as a minister in the Church. The list given, although much shorter, has similarities to the list provided for overseers but adds in verse ten: "... these men must first be tested...". It is paramount that people placed in such responsible roles must first be tested. It is rather short-sighted to put people in leadership positions only to discover later that they were not adequately prepared nor have the maturity for the position. So, by then, it is too late.

Leadership competency

In the rest of society, we would expect any professional person we went to for a particular service to be adequately qualified and experienced in their expertise. We expect them to be well trained and hold the necessary qualifications regarding the field they are working in. They may be doctors, nurses, counsellors, dentists, solicitors, social workers, financial advisors, surgeons, accountants, plumbers, electricians, or builders, etc. Irrespective of their discipline, we would want to be confident that they have a good work ethic and, in some instances, able to obtain references from other customers or be assured that they are part of an established reputable organisation.

We would not find it acceptable to discover that the person has little experience or inadequate qualification for their role, or even if they did have, that their work ethic was highly questionable and marred by a history of professional misconduct. We have the recourse in some instances to initiate legal action, which may cause criminal charges being brought against them and compensation for damages we may have suffered in any way. They may even be prohibited from working in that field, and in some circumstances, be criminally convicted and incarcerated.

Unfortunately, when it comes to the things of God, for the most part, people seem to hold church leaders to a much lower standard. This is because we make assumptions based upon many other criteria other than the most important one, their character. The Bible clarifies that we can only truly know an individual by the fruit of their character:

> *"Beware of false prophets, who come to you in sheep's clothing, but inwardly they are ravenous wolves. You will know them by their fruits. Do men gather grapes from thornbushes or figs from thistles? Even so, every good tree bears good fruit, but a bad tree bears bad fruit. A good tree cannot bear bad fruit, nor can a bad tree bear good fruit. Every tree that does not bear good fruit is cut down and thrown into the fire. Therefore by their fruits you will know them* (**Matthew 7:15-20**; *NKJV*).

Although the above verse specifically mentions false prophets, we should apply the same principles of discernment to anyone in the capacity of church leadership. First, notice it says, "...but inwardly they are ravenous wolves". It is easy for a person to pretend they are someone else because of their title, position, or who they are associated with, but their real identity can be seen in their character.

It is essential that leaders have adequate training and experience to fulfil their roles. The apostle Paul advises young Timothy in his handling and teaching of God's word: *Study and do your best to present yourself to God approved, a workman [tested by trial] who has no reason to be ashamed, accurately handling and skilfully teaching the word of truth* (**2 Timothy 2:15**; AMP).

Leaders with the responsibility of looking after people's souls should have, as a bare minimum, basic training in their area of calling, be it biblical theology, counselling, or possess relevant and transferable skills that complement their role. It is not just a matter of having the anointing but mentoring and training are also essential to the success of their leadership role. Jesus spent three and a half years closely discipling His disciples and poured a great deal into them, which became evident after His ascension near the day of Pentecost.

The role of leadership

The Bible enables us to properly understand God's perspective on the role leadership must play in the Body of Christ:

> *And He Himself gave some to be apostles, some prophets, some evangelists, and some pastors and teachers, for the equipping of the saints for the work of ministry, for the edifying of the body of Christ, till we all come to the unity of the faith and of the knowledge of the Son of God, to a perfect man, to the measure of the stature of the fullness of Christ (***Ephesians 4:11-13****; NKJV).*

The role of the five-fold ministry; apostles, prophets, evangelists, pastors, and teachers are to equip the saints so that they can grow and get on with doing the work of the ministry. It is a role that facilitates the maturing of believers so they can understand the part they must play in building up the wider Body of Christ. This would include any ministry that will enable people to be delivered and healed from negative spiritual things that have afflicted them during their lives. This is to make their minds become transformed and freed. It will make them think and behave in ways conducive to building a thriving, powerful Holy Spirit-led body of believers, the Church.

Now, edifying the Body of Christ is an act of building up, improving, enriching, and educating people in ways that do not cause harm. It is the leadership's role to promote the growth of those they lead in Christian wisdom, happiness, and holiness. So, the role of leadership is to equip the saints to do the work of the ministry, serve, and bring edification to the Body of Christ. Leadership is there to serve the Church, <u>NOT</u> the other way around. It is a selfless, sacrificial role, as Jesus Himself demonstrated.

God's expectations of His leaders

God places leaders in our lives to guide, support, protect, nurture, and feed us spiritually. They are expected to have good moral standards and live a life of integrity. This is what God expects from His leaders, and so should we. By understanding the biblical standards set out in scripture for leaders, we will be able to see clearly when a leader deviates from them. It is God's divine order for us to be submitted to godly leadership, so we need to be aware of what kind of person we are submitting ourselves to. Problems occur when people unwittingly submit themselves to the authority of leaders that are not truly representing our Heavenly Father. Godly leadership has a very significant role to play in the life of the Church and the discipling of believers, which is why He expects us to submit to their God-given authority as our leaders.

Why should we submit to church leaders? You may be asking, and the answer can be found in the following verse: *Obey those who rule over you, and be submissive, for they watch out for your souls, as those who must give account* (**Hebrews 13:17**; NKJV). It is scriptural for us to submit to godly leadership, as they have a significant role in our lives and will one day give an account to God for how they operated in their roles. However, God does not expect us to submit ourselves to abusive leaders who are detrimental to our spiritual well-being and relationship with Him. Therefore, it is dangerous to remain submitted under a leadership that is spiritually harmful to us or others.

Kingdom Leadership

Kingdom leadership is different from leadership in the world, and there should be a noticeable distinction between the two. In Matthew 20, the mother of the two disciples, James and John, approaches Jesus, asking Him if her two sons could be given positions of honour and authority in His Kingdom. However, He responds that positions in the Kingdom are not given by Him but only by His Father in heaven:

> *Then the mother of Zebedee's sons came to Him with her sons, kneeling down and asking something from Him. And He said to her, "What do you wish?" She said to Him, "Grant that these two sons of mine may sit, one on Your right hand and the other on the left, in Your kingdom." But Jesus answered and said, "You do not know what you ask. Are you able to drink the cup that I am about to drink, and be baptized with the baptism that I am baptized with?" They said to Him, "We are able." So, He said to them, "You will indeed drink My cup, and be baptized with the baptism that I am baptized with; but to sit on My right hand and on My left is not Mine to give, but it is for those for whom it is prepared by My Father." And when the ten heard it, they were greatly displeased with the two brothers (***Matthew 20:20-24****; NKJV*).*

The disciples were understandably upset with the two brothers and their request for an elevated position in the Kingdom alongside Jesus Christ. However, Jesus does not address their misgivings about the request but begins to explain to them what true kingdom leadership looks like:

> *But Jesus called them to Himself and said,*
> *"You know that the rulers of the Gentiles lord*
> *it over them, and those who are great exercise*
> *authority over them. Yet it shall not be so*
> *among you; but whoever desires to become*
> *great among you, let him be your servant.*
> *And whoever desires to be first among you,*
> *let him be your slave—just as the Son of Man*
> *did not come to be served, but to serve, and to*
> *give His life a ransom for many"* (**Matthew**
> **20:25-28**; *NKJV*).

The principles of the world encourage a different form of leadership and are more focused on leading than serving the people. So, Jesus explained to the disciples that the Kingdom of God operates differently and, therefore, should not emulate the leadership of the world. In other words, a godly leader needs to be prepared to serve others with humility.

Kingdom leadership was not about having recognised positions of honour and authority, but a leader in God's kingdom must be willing to serve. They must have a servant-hearted attitude and be ready to serve others, not for others to be serving them. He gave them a clear Kingdom template for how a leader should operate within the Kingdom of God. Let's have a look at those verses again in the Amplified version:

> *But Jesus called them to Himself and said,*
> *"You know that the rulers of the Gentiles*
> *have absolute power and lord it over them,*
> *and their great men exercise authority over*
> *them [tyrannizing them]. It is not this way*
> *among you, but whoever wishes to become*
> *great among you shall be your servant, and*
> *whoever wishes to be first among you shall be*

> *your [willing and humble] slave; just as the*
> *Son of Man did not come to be served, but to*
> *serve, and to give His life as a ransom for many*
> *[paying the price to set them free from the*
> *penalty of sin]"* **(Matthew 20:25-28; AMP).**

Here, Jesus was drawing a clear contrast between the two types of leadership. Gentile's or the world's leadership have an attitude that lords it over those they lead. It is overpowering and oppressive. It is a manipulative, bullying form of leadership that has absolutely nothing to do with leadership principles in God's Kingdom.

On the other hand, leadership in the Kingdom of God is the exact opposite; great godly leadership equates to humbly serving others, as quoted in verse 26: "...whosoever will be great among you, let him be your minister..." a servant (**Matthew 20:26**; KJV).

One type of leadership is a harsh, controlling form of leadership, but the other is leadership that humbly serves others. Therefore, godly leadership should never exhibit the characteristics that Jesus mentions about gentile or worldly leadership. It should never be manipulative, controlling, or domineering, which is abusive.

Servant Leadership

Jesus took time to explain to His disciples the kind of leadership that reflected Kingdom values so they could emulate it further down the line. It was essential to their role as apostles to understand this because it sets a precedent for others to follow.

> *Jesus, knowing that the Father had given all*
> *things into His hands, and that He had come*
> *from God and was going to God, rose from*

*supper and laid aside His garments, took a towel and girded Himself. After that, He poured water into a basin and began to wash the disciples' feet, and to wipe them with the towel with which He was girded. Then He came to Simon Peter. And Peter said to Him, "Lord, are You washing my feet?" Jesus answered and said to him, "What I am doing you do not understand now, but you will know after this." Peter said to Him, "You shall never wash my feet! "Jesus answered him, "If I do not wash you, you have no part with Me." Simon Peter said to Him, "Lord, not my feet only, but also my hands and my head!" Jesus said to him, "He who is bathed needs only to wash his feet, but is completely clean; and you are clean, but not all of you." For He knew who would betray Him; therefore He said, "You are not all clean." So when He had washed their feet, taken His garments, and sat down again, He said to them, "Do you know what I have done to you? You call Me Teacher and Lord, and you say well, for so I am. If I then, your Lord and Teacher, have washed your feet, you also ought to wash one another's feet. For I have given you an example, that you should do as I have done to you (**John 13:3-15;** NKJV).*

In those days, it was the servant's job to wash the feet of visitors coming into the house. The streets were dusty, and the feet would become sweaty and dirty. The feet were regarded as the filthiest part of the body, so for Jesus to get down on His knees and wash the feet of the disciples was strange for them to experience. After all, He was their Lord and master, and here, He was acting like a servant. One of the reasons leaders can cause great hurt to congregants is that they may never have properly understood that their role is to serve others.

Lack of biblical understanding may mean they view "strong" leadership similarly to the leadership Jesus warned against. It is a blessing to be able to bless and support our leaders, but leaders who demand that congregants "serve" them may have ulterior motives.

Addressing Issues

Another important aspect of Kingdom leadership is a leader's willingness to confront issues, no matter how uncomfortable or difficult they may be. It is their role to protect congregants from things that have the potential to negatively affect other congregants or destroy a ministry if not dealt with appropriately. Any leader that cannot address issues in line with Kingdom values is not doing their job description. As a shepherd, they are there to protect the flock, be aware of wolves, discern impending danger, and take appropriate corrective action. The Apostle Paul immediately addresses a grave matter in the verse below as soon as it comes to his attention:

> *It is actually reported that there is sexual immorality among you, and such sexual immorality as is not even named among the Gentiles—that a man has his father's wife! And you are puffed up, and have not rather mourned, that he who has done this deed might be taken away from among you* (**1 Corinthians 5:1-2**; *NKJV*).

Once Paul discovers what is going on in the Corinthian church, he immediately addresses it full on. He highlights their lackadaisical attitude in failing to address the problem, the action that needs to be taken, and the spiritual consequences of the effect on the entire congregation if the problem is not removed.

> *Deliver such a one to Satan for the destruction of the flesh, that his spirit may be saved in the day of the Lord Jesus. Your glorying is not good. Do you not know that a little leaven leavens the whole lump? Therefore purge out the old leaven, that you may be a new lump, since you truly are unleavened. For indeed Christ, our Passover, was sacrificed for us. Therefore let us keep the feast, not with old leaven, nor with the leaven of malice and wickedness, but with the unleavened bread of sincerity and truth (***1 Corinthians 5:5-8***; NKJV).*

He reminds them about sexual immorality in their congregation and the parameters that should be in place concerning other issues that can cause major problems in the church if not addressed adequately and for their need to act immediately.

> *I wrote to you in my epistle not to keep company with sexually immoral people. Yet I certainly did not mean with the sexually immoral people of this world, or with the covetous, or extortioners, or idolaters, since then you would need to go out of the world. But now I have written to you not to keep company with anyone named a brother, who is sexually*

> *immoral, or covetous, or an idolater, or a reviler, or a drunkard, or an extortioner—not even to eat with such a person. For what have I to do with judging those also who are outside? Do you not judge those who are inside? But those who are outside God judges. Therefore "put away from yourselves the evil person"* (**1 Corinthians 5:9-13;** *NKJV*).

The Apostle Paul was more than willing and able to address issues that had the potential to defile the Church and was very clear about what should be done in such circumstances. He was concerned about the spiritual well-being of not just the individual, but the entire congregation. He recognised the potential danger of this situation not being effectively dealt with swiftly and therefore gave explicit instructions about what needed to be done.

A leader who is unable to adequately address issues leaves the congregation vulnerable, making the potential for the issue to get worse and spread throughout the entire group. Much like cancer that needs to be cut out of the body to save the entire body, a leader must be able to confront issues and take appropriate action. Colluding with sin issues out of fear or compromising the standards of God's Kingdom can have dire consequences.

Compassionate leadership

As well as dealing with challenging issues, a leader must also be able to show compassion and a willingness to work with even the most difficult individuals. This can be achieved wherever there is a desire on the person's behalf to engage with the process of repentance, deliverance, restoration, and inner healing.

*For out of much affliction and anguish of heart
I wrote to you, with many tears, not that you
should be grieved, but that you might know the
love which I have so abundantly for you. But
if anyone has caused grief, he has not grieved
me, but all of you to some extent—not to be too
severe. This punishment which was inflicted
by the majority is sufficient for such a man,
so that, on the contrary, you ought rather to
forgive and comfort him, lest perhaps such a
one be swallowed up with too much sorrow.
Therefore I urge you to reaffirm your love to
him (**2 Corinthians 2:4-8**; NKJV).*

Although Paul dealt with issues, he was also compassionate and caring towards those who had previously done wrong. He cared about the soul of the person who had been disciplined and wanted him to be restored into the fold. Likewise, godly leadership should lovingly and compassionately be willing to restore those who have messed up but are repentant and remorseful.

Kingdom leadership is essential to the healthy growth of the Body of Christ. God's leaders should always be clearly different from the world's leadership style, as they are God's representatives. Misunderstanding Kingdom leadership can lead to spiritual abuse and hurt many people in the Body of Christ. So, in summary, from a biblical perspective, godly leadership should be characterised by the following.

1. Leadership should be educated, trained, or mentored for their role, e.g., theological training, counselling training, etc., or have relevant transferable skills and experience

2. Their responsibility is to equip the saints to do the work of the ministry

3. Their objective must always be to edify the Body of Christ—build others up and promote their growth

4. They must have God's heart towards His people—they should genuinely love people

5. They should be able to teach, and their teaching needs to be biblically sound

6. They must have integrity and reverently fear God

7. They should serve their congregants and lead with humility

8. They must not be manipulative, controlling, or domineering

9. They must be able to address sin issues in the congregation, biblically

10. They must be compassionate and loving

Chapter 2

Ungodly Leadership

False Leaders

God used prophets throughout the Old Testament to speak to His people on His behalf but also anticipated there would be false prophets attempting to influence His people simultaneously. So, the phenomenon of false leaders has existed for thousands of years. Let us look at what God has to say about such leaders:

> *I will raise up for them a Prophet like you from among their brethren, and will put My words in His mouth, and He shall speak to them all that I command Him. And it shall be that whoever will not hear My words, which He speaks in My name, I will require it of him. But the prophet who presumes to speak a word in My name, which I have not commanded him to speak, or who speaks in the name of other gods, that prophet shall die* (**Deuteronomy 18:18-20**; *NKJV*).

These Old Testament scriptures highlight that in those days, some people with the prophetic ministry were doing their own thing; therefore, God warned them of the dire consequences. The prophet Jeremiah was an authentic Old

Testament prophet used by God to pronounce judgement at certain times. Judgement was about to fall on Jerusalem because of their sinful ways, and God highlights the reasons through His prophet Jeremiah:

> *"Because from the least of them even to the greatest of them, Everyone is given to covetousness; And from the prophet even to the priest, Everyone deals falsely. They have also healed the hurt of My people slightly, Saying, 'Peace, peace!' When there is no peace.*
> **(Jeremiah 6:13-14**; *NKJV)*

God highlights the reasons for the impending judgement

- The priests and prophets used their positions inappropriately.
- They were motivated by greed.
- They offered the people false hope and ineffective solutions to their problems.

God places the responsibility for the impending judgement clearly on the heads of the false leaders. They were the reason the people would suffer judgment, and it was a consequence of following leaders who did not obey God. Later, God instructed the prophet Jeremiah to pronounce judgement over the people:

> *Thus says the Lord to this people: "Thus they have loved to wander, They have not restrained their feet. Therefore, the Lord does not accept them; He will remember their iniquity now and punish their sins." Then the Lord said to me, "Do not pray for this people, for their good. When*

33

> *they fast, I will not hear their cry; and when they offer burnt offering and grain offering, I will not accept them. But I will consume them by the sword, by the famine, and by the pestilence (Jeremiah 14:10-12; NKJV).*

The judgement was directed at not only the leaders but the people who followed them. Although God made it very clear about the judgement He was about to execute, the false prophets continued with their own agenda and misrepresented God to the people:

> *Then I said, "Ah, Lord God! Behold the prophets say to them, 'You shall not see the sword, nor shall you have famine, but I will give you assured peace in this place.'" And the Lord said to me, "The prophets prophesy lies in My name. I have not sent them, commanded them, nor spoken to them; they prophesy to you a false vision, divination, a worthless thing, and the deceit of their heart (Jeremiah 14:13-14; NKJV).*

The Amplified version describes verse 14 this way: *"... They prophesy to you a false or pretended vision, a worthless divination [conjuring or practicing magic, trying to call forth the responses supposed to be given by idols].*

The false prophets were:
- Seeking information through occultic practices, which was clearly against God's law.
- Using demonic powers.
- Saying the exact opposite of what God had said through the prophet Jeremiah.

- Making things up out of their own minds.

Any leader seeking after and using any power other than the Holy Spirit is NOT of God and has ventured into the demonic realm. **Note**: if you have ever submitted to a leader using demonic powers for any reason, you too may have come under the influence of demons. In a later chapter, we will examine how to break free from satanic influences following spiritually abusive situations.

Let's continue the story in Jeremiah 14. After Jeremiah told the people God's message about impending judgement, the false prophets told the people something contrary to God's words:

> *Therefore, thus says the Lord concerning the prophets who prophesy in My name, who I did not send, and who say, 'Sword and famine shall not be in this land'—'By sword and famine those prophets shall be consumed! And the people to whom they prophesy shall be cast out in the streets of Jerusalem because of famine and the sword; they will have no one to bury them— them nor their wives, their sons nor their daughters—for I will pour their wickedness on them." (**Jeremiah 14:15-16**; NKJV).*

So far, we have learned three things from Old Testament examples about false prophets:

1. Just because someone has a position and a title does NOT mean they are truly of God.
2. A false leader may not have God-given authority, but they can still influence others negatively.

3. Taking counsel or advice from false leaders may have serious consequences.

Let's look at some more encounters with false leaders by the prophet Jeremiah and see what he has to say about them and their character:

> *Also, I have seen a horrible thing in the prophets of Jerusalem: They commit adultery and walk in lies; They also strengthen the hands of evildoers, So that no one turns back from his wickedness. All of them are like Sodom to Me, And her inhabitants like Gomorrah* (**Jeremiah 23:14**; *NKJV*).

These scriptures are telling us that for the false prophet,

- Their sinful and immoral lifestyles were at odds with the calling of an authentic prophet.
- Anything they said could not be trusted.
- They encourage others to sin and support evil.
- Their actions exposed who they truly were.
- Titles do not tell us the true character of an individual.

Although there were many authentic prophets during those times, we have many others who had such titles but were not instructed by God. Micah was another authentic God-ordained prophet who also encountered false prophets during his day:

> *Some false prophets are telling lies to the Lord's people. This is what the Lord says about them: "These prophets are led by their stomachs. They promise peace for those who*

*give them food, but they promise war to those
who do not give them food. "This is why it is
like night for you and you don't have visions.
You cannot see what will happen in the future,
so it is like darkness to you. The sun has gone
down on the prophets. They cannot see what
will happen in the future, so it is like darkness
to them. The seers are ashamed. The fortune
tellers are embarrassed. None of them will say
anything because God will not speak to them"*
(Micah 3:5-7; *ERV).*

According to this passage, the false prophets were:

1. Telling lies to the people.
2. Led by their stomachs—motivated by what they could get from the people.
3. Not able to see into the future.
4. Would be ashamed and embarrassed.
5. Not hearing from God—He was not speaking to them.

Let's look at some other leaders found in the Old Testament. Israel is often described in scripture as a flock and their appointed leaders as shepherds who were to care for God's people. Ezekiel was another God-ordained prophet who warned the leaders set over the people of Israel:

*And the word of the Lord came to me, saying,
"Son of man, prophesy against the shepherds
of Israel, prophesy and say to them, 'Thus
says the Lord God to the shepherds: "Woe to
the shepherds of Israel who feed themselves!*

Should not the shepherds feed the flocks? You eat the fat and clothe yourselves with the wool; you slaughter the fatlings, but you do not feed the flock. The weak you have not strengthened, nor have you healed those who were sick, nor bound up the broken, nor brought back what was driven away, nor sought what was lost; but with force and cruelty you have ruled them (**Ezekiel 34:1-4**; *NKJV*).

Effectively, the irresponsible leaders in Israel were doing their own thing:

- They fed themselves
- They used the people
- Do not care for the weak & sick
- Do not have interest in those who had wandered
- No interest in the lost
- Led with force and cruelty

Let's jump down to Ezekiel 34:16 (NKJV): "*I will seek what was lost and bring back what was driven away, bind up the broken and strengthen what was sick; but I will destroy the fat and the strong, and feed them in judgment.*"

God never took the mistreatment and abuse of His people lightly. There were always consequences for the leadership responsible for mistreating His people.

In the next scenario, the prophet Isaiah warns Samaria about the impending destruction directly resulting from the corrupt leadership:

Therefore, the Lord will cut off head and tail from Israel, Palm branch and bulrush in one

day. The elder and honourable, he is the head;
The prophet who teaches lies, he is the tail. For
the leaders of this people cause them to err,
And those who are led by them are destroyed
(Isaiah 9:14-16; *NKJV).*

The people suffered because they submitted themselves to ungodly leadership with personal agendas who did not care about the well-being of God's people. It was a regular theme throughout the Old Testament, and God always intervened at some point, bringing judgement on the heads of those responsible. Consequently, those they were leading also suffered hurt and harm because of their submission to the authority of corrupt leadership.

False Leaders Today

It can be quite shocking when we hear of spiritually abusive situations or personally experience them ourselves. It can take us by surprise, and all kinds of questions may come to mind, such as, how can this kind of thing happen in the Church? How can leaders do such evil and cause so much harm? Why do people stay in such situations? It can seriously damage a person's relationship with God and shatter their faith in many ways. It may even cause some to erroneously believe that Satan is far more powerful than God. As a result, the person will point to various instances of hurtful church situations as "evidence". Sadly, it also gives others the excuse not to want anything to do with churches or God whatsoever.

The reality is that nothing surprises God, not instances of spiritual abuse. Even though He is not the orchestrator, His word tells us that these things will happen in our world, even amongst those professing the Christian faith, just as it happened centuries ago amongst His followers. Believers today are not immune to such experiences. By understanding the warnings the word of God gives us, we will be better able to avoid such unhealthy situations that may happen within the context of Christian Church groups or organisations. We will be better equipped to hopefully avoid finding ourselves in such situations. However, even if we experience them, we'll be adequately able to find a way out and seek refuge in a place of healing and restoration.

The Bible is a unique book in the world because it is God speaking to us through its pages. Moreover, biblical scholars and theologians have realised that about one-third of the scriptures are prophetic; they give us insight into future events before they happen. The scripture below confirms this for us:

> *So, we have the prophetic word made more certain. You do well to pay [close] attention to it as to a lamp shining in a dark place, until the day dawns and light breaks through the gloom and the morning star arises in your hearts. But understand this first of all, that no prophecy of Scripture is a matter of or comes from one's own [personal or special] interpretation, for no prophecy was ever made by an act of human will, but men moved by the Holy Spirit spoke from God (***2 Peter 1:19-21***; AMP).*

> *God used people to reveal things that would happen hundreds or thousands of years before their time. He wanted those living in that future epoch to recognise the times they were living in. Now, let's turn our attention to scriptures to discover the prophetic words*

written about false leaders and spiritually abusive situations in the context of the church today. The following verses in 1 Timothy are known as "The Great Apostasy" or the great falling away from the Christian faith: Now the Spirit expressly says that in latter times some will depart from the faith, giving heed to deceiving spirits and doctrines of demons... (**1 Timothy 4:1**; *NKJV*).

The phrase "latter times" is sometimes translated in other versions of the Bible as "last days", "last times", or "end times". This period is between the Holy Spirit's outpouring on the day of Pentecost (around AD 33) and Jesus Christ's return, which is still yet to happen as of the writing of this book. So, the period we live in at this precise moment is the latter times:

Now the Spirit expressly says that in latter times some will depart from the faith, giving heed to deceiving spirits and doctrines of demons, speaking lies in hypocrisy, having their own conscience seared with a hot iron, forbidding to marry, and commanding to abstain from foods which God created to be received with thanksgiving by those who believe and know the truth (**1 Timothy 4:1-3**; *NKJV*).

Although the above verses do not explicitly mention the word "leaders", the fact that some of them are "forbidding" and "commanding" tells us they have influence and control over others within the Church context. It also highlights some key pointers about specific things we can expect to see relating to false leaders during this period.

41

- False teachers influenced by demons
- Spreading false doctrine
- Speaking lies in hypocrisy—falsehood, duplicity, pretence, insincerity
- Conscience seared with a hot iron—damaged conscience: Incapable of ethical functioning
- Implementing outlandish practices contrary to God's word

These things above will tell us they are false leaders; therefore, we should steer clear of them because of our spiritual well-being. The Apostle Peter also gives us insight into the characteristics of false leaders in our time:

> But there were also false prophets among the people, even as there will be false teachers among you, who will secretly bring in destructive heresies, even denying the Lord who bought them, and bring on themselves swift destruction. And many will follow their destructive ways, because of whom the way of truth will be blasphemed. By covetousness they will exploit you with deceptive words; for a long time, their judgment has not been idle, and their destruction does not slumber (**2 Peter 2:1-3**; *NKJV*).

Peter is warning the Church that just as there were false prophets in the past, there will be false teachers in the end-time Church. So, let's look at those verses again, but in the Living Bible version:

> But there were false prophets, too, in those days, just as there will be false teachers among

*you. They will cleverly tell their lies about God, turning against even their Master who bought them; but theirs will be a swift and terrible end. Many will follow their evil teaching that there is nothing wrong with sexual sin. And because of them Christ and his way will be scoffed at. These teachers in their greed will tell you anything to get hold of your money. But God condemned them long ago and their destruction is on the way (***2 Peter 2:1-3***; TLB).*

Here, Peter is highlighting four indicators of false teachers:

- They will bring in destructive heresies (unorthodox religious opinion).
- They will have large followings that believe their lies about sexual sin being fine.
- They will deceive people and financially exploit them.
- They will cause others to disrespect God.

Later in the same chapter, Peter gives even more prophetic insight into the types of behaviours that will be evident amongst false teachers:

For uttering arrogant words of vanity [pompous words disguised to sound scholarly or profound, but meaning nothing and containing no spiritual truth], they beguile and lure using lustful desires, by sensuality, those who barely escape from the ones who live in error. They promise them liberty, when they themselves are the slaves of depravity—for by whatever anyone is defeated and overcome, to that [person, thing, philosophy, or concept] he is continually enslaved. For if, after they have escaped the pollutions of the world by [personal] knowledge of our Lord and Saviour Jesus Christ, they are again entangled in them and are overcome, their last condition has become worse for them than the first. For it would have been better for them not to have [personally] known the way of righteousness, than to have known it and then to have turned back from the holy commandment [verbally] handed on to them. The thing spoken of in the true proverb has happened to them, "The dog returns to his own vomit," and, "A sow is washed only to wallow [again] in the mire" (**2 Peter 2:18-22**; *AMP*).

Characteristics of false leaders in the end times:

- Great speaking abilities which captivate audiences, but their words have no spiritual substance.
- They hypocritically offer hope of freedom to others whilst they themselves are slaves to depraved and defiling lifestyles.
- They once knew the truth but have returned to their former ways.

The Book of Jude also gives us insight into behaviours that will be evident amongst false leaders in our times:

Dearly loved friends, I had been planning to write you some thoughts about the salvation God has given us, but now I find I must write of something else instead, urging you to stoutly

defend the truth that God gave once for all to
his people to keep without change through the
years. I say this because some godless teachers
have wormed their way in among you, saying
that after we become Christians we can do just
as we like without fear of God's punishment.
The fate of such people was written long ago,
for they have turned against our only Master
and Lord, Jesus Christ...that in the last times
there would come these scoffers whose whole
purpose in life is to enjoy themselves in every
*evil way imaginable (**Jude 3-4, 18**; TLB).*

Both Peter & Jude warned of the deception creeping into the churches during their time. Individuals would be:

- Sneaking into the churches with ulterior motives.
- Bringing in destructive heresies.
- Encouraging believers to embrace immoral lifestyles under the guise of "Grace".
- Lacking the Spirit of God and causing divisions.

We are at the same end time and therefore seeing the same things nowadays as they saw in the early church.

But understand this, that in the last days
dangerous times [of great stress and trouble]
will come [difficult days that will be hard
to bear]. For people will be lovers of self
[narcissistic, self-focused], lovers of money
[impelled by greed], boastful, arrogant, revilers,
disobedient to parents, ungrateful, unholy and
profane, [and they will be] unloving [devoid
of natural human affection, calloused and

> *inhumane], irreconcilable, malicious gossips,*
> *devoid of self-control [intemperate, immoral],*
> *brutal, haters of good, traitors, reckless,*
> *conceited, lovers of [sensual] pleasure rather*
> *than lovers of God (***2 Timothy 3:1-4***; AMP).*

Paul clearly describes from verses 1-4 the state of our world in the end times. However, when we read verse five, it reveals the context in which the behaviour of those he has mentioned is taking place:

> *For [although] they hold a form of piety*
> *(true religion), they deny and reject and are*
> *strangers to the power of it [their conduct*
> *belies the genuineness of their profession].*
> *Avoid [all] such people [turn away from them*
> *(***2 Timothy 3:5***; Amp).*

These people are merely looking the part, whilst at the same time exhibiting attitudes and behaviours contrary to the life of true believers. So prophetically, the scriptures have established that, during the end times, individuals in religious settings will have their own ungodly agenda. It will merely be a case of them looking the part from an outward perspective. However, their motives and agenda within the religious setting are self-centred and have nothing to do with God.

So, having established that the issue of false leaders and spiritually abusive situations within the context of religious environments are regular occurrences during the end times, our times, how can we avoid such situations when we notice the characteristics of false leaders within our midst? The Book of Matthew gives a clue to how to recognise false leaders:

"Beware of false prophets who come disguised as harmless sheep but are really vicious wolves. You can identify them by their fruit, that is, by the way they act. Can you pick grapes from thornbushes, or figs from thistles? A good tree produces good fruit, and a bad tree produces bad fruit. A good tree can't produce bad fruit, and a bad tree can't produce good fruit. So every tree that does not produce good fruit is chopped down and thrown into the fire. Yes, just as you can identify a tree by its fruit, so you can identify people by their actions (**Matthew 7:15-20**; *NLT*).

The word of God says we only really know people by their fruit, meaning what they say and do, in other words, their character. Therefore, we should never be taken in by someone simply because of,

- speaking ability
- title or position
- congregation size
- financial status
- education
- spiritual gifting
- ability to pull a crowd and raise large offerings, etc.

It is imperative for our own as well as others' safety that we correctly discern a person's character before submitting to their leadership and testing things out. There may be dire consequences for failing to do this, and the scripture tells us that this is something we should do: *Beloved, do not believe every spirit, but test the spirits, whether they are of God, because many false prophets have gone out into the world (1 John 4:1; NKJV).*

So therefore, we shouldn't simply accept someone as a prophet or a leader just because they or others say they are. We will only truly know a leader by their fruit (behaviour and actions). False leaders are a part of the reality that we must face in the twenty-first-century church, just as they did in times past. It is inevitable, but we shouldn't fall victim to what the enemy desires to do through them, i.e., hurting God's people. They will suffer the consequences of the evil they have done, but God will not necessarily remove them instantly as much as we would like Him to. As the following verses illustrate, this could potentially cause other true believers to also be uprooted and harmed:

> *Jesus gave them another parable [to consider], saying, "The kingdom of heaven is like a man who sowed good seed in his field. But while his men were sleeping, his enemy came and sowed weeds [resembling wheat] among the wheat and went away. So when the plants sprouted and formed grain, the weeds appeared also. The servants of the owner came to him and said, 'Sir, did you not sow good seed in your field? Then how does it have weeds in it?' He replied to them, 'An enemy has done this.' The servants asked him, 'Then do you want us to go and pull them out?' But he said, 'No; because as you pull out the weeds, you may uproot the wheat with them. Let them grow together until the harvest; and at harvest time I will tell the reapers, "First gather the weeds and tie them*

*in bundles to be burned; but gather the wheat into my barn"' (**Matthew 13:24-30**; AMP).*

The reality is there will always be those who profess to be of God but are not. However, God has warned us through the scriptures about false leaders appearing in the Church in these end times. He has also given us wisdom, discernment, and His Word to highlight signs of potential danger for us. Ultimately, false leaders will reap what they have sown unless there is true repentance, and we can trust God to protect us when we are obedient to His directions and promptings.

Let's end by summarising ten key points to take note of:

1. In today's Church, there are false leaders, false prophets, and false teachers. It is inevitable!

2. Titles and positions do not tell us who a person really is, but their character will.

3. A false leader may not have God-given authority, but they can still negatively influence others.

4. Taking counsel or advice from false leaders can have grave consequences.

5. A leader may have a position of authority but be influenced by demons.

6. The enemy uses false leaders to bring destructive heresies (unbiblical teaching).

7. False leaders may encourage believers to embrace an immoral lifestyle under the guise of "Grace".

8. Unscrupulous leaders have no conscience and may place unscriptural burdens on others.

9. A false leader may have great speaking abilities but have no spiritual substance to their words.

10. God never takes the mistreatment and abuse of His people lightly and will do something about it in due course.

Chapter 3

Eleven signs of abusive churches and leadership

We have established so far that false leaders, false prophets, and false teachers are a necessary evil in our times. Now, how can we avoid abusive leadership and abusive churches? What kinds of things should we look out for that may be cause for concern? No church organisation or group is perfect, and you may notice things you are unhappy about, but that does not mean you are in an abusive church or a particular leader is a false leader.

What we are talking about are situations that are consistently abusive to people under the guise of "strong leadership" or "obeying leadership". These are situations where people are not encouraged to think for themselves, and if they felt the need to highlight concerns or problems, they will be labelled as being the problem. It can also be circumstances where people are made to feel as though they cannot properly hear from God or make personal life decisions without the approval of their leaders.

We will look at eleven signs that could indicate an abusive church or false leadership. Of course, this does not mean any individual point is proof by itself, but several indicators may be a serious cause for concern.

1. Excessive time in church at the expense of important relationships

There is nothing wrong with attending church meetings besides our time of weekly corporate worship and even prayer meetings, but do you feel unable to say no to attending certain meetings? Are you made to feel that you are not adequately supporting the group because you cannot attend every meeting? Are scriptures like the one below used to make you feel guilty for missing certain meetings? *Not forsaking the assembling of ourselves together, as is the manner of some, but exhorting one another, and so much the more as you see the Day approaching (***Hebrews 10:25***; NKJV).*

This scripture is often manipulated to make people feel guilty about not attending every meeting. Church attendance is crucial, but not to the extent where other areas of your life are suffering because of it. For example, your relationships with family and friends may dwindle because of your commitment to attending every meeting. It could be that the time you previously spent exercising, doing hobbies, and doing things to relax is constantly put on the back burner. The key thing here is balance. God is not expecting anyone to allow relationships vital to our emotional and mental well-being to suffer because we feel guilty about not being part of a particular group's activities every time they hold a meeting. Any group that puts pressure on us and causes us to feel guilty for having a healthy balanced life is controlling and detrimental to our overall mental and emotional health and certainly not in line with a positive environment conducive to our spiritual well-being.

2. Pressure to give financially

Giving to the work of God is crucial and totally scriptural. Many believe in tithing, which is fine. However, besides the tithe, we should feel free to give whatever free-will offerings we choose in our hearts. Paul has this to say in Corinthians, *But this I say: He who sows sparingly will also reap sparingly, and he who sows bountifully will also reap bountifully* (**2 Corinthians 9:6**; *NKJV*).

This scripture is often used to encourage people to give with no emphasis on the next verse, which talks about the attitude in which we should give: *So, let each one give as he purposes in his heart, not grudgingly or of necessity; for God loves a cheerful giver* (**2 Corinthians 9:7**; *NKJV*).

Notice the words "*purposes in his heart*" and "*not grudgingly or of necessity*". There is nothing wrong with leadership raising offerings for special projects or supporting a genuine need, but there may be times when you honestly cannot or simply do not feel like you should give. God would not expect us to put ourselves in debt or damage our credit to give. Whatever a person gives should be because they are genuinely happy to do so and not out of guilt, fear, or feelings that God will punish them somehow. If you are not giving in faith, you cannot give cheerfully. Ultimately, YOU are the one who determines the offering you will give, not anybody else.

If you are married and share finances, you should consult your spouse first, especially if it comes from a joint account. Ultimately, as an individual, you should determine in your own heart how much you would like to give without feeling obligated or coerced into it. Sometimes, a person feels a genuine prompting from God to give, but that amount should ultimately be determined by your personal relationship with God, not through pressure.

3. Ungodly treatment of congregants/members

It is God's will for us to obey godly leaders, but often, the mere fact that someone has a recognised title or position within a Church context is given as a good reason to blindly follow everything they say. A scripture often used out of context to coerce people to conform to every rule of leadership is in the Book of Hebrews: *Obey those who rule over you, and be submissive, for they watch out for your souls, as those who must give account. Let them do so with joy and not with grief, for that would be unprofitable for you (***Hebrews 13:17***; NKJV).*

God would not require you to obey an abusive leader who is hurting you or encouraging you to sin in some way. Just because a person is "ruling" over us does not mean we must obey things they say or do that are clearly not in line with God's standards for His people.

Some Indicators of abusive treatment:

a) "Members/Congregants" commanded to consult leadership about personal private matters. Are people made to feel they must consult their leadership about personal private matters, e.g., moving house or location, having children, going on holiday, changing jobs, etc.?

b) Promoting or creating a culture of ungodly "reverence" and loyalty towards the leader. Treating the leader like a god and being fearful of them and what they say. We are not talking about genuine healthy respect for godly leaders, which is scriptural, but a culture of idolatry and ungodly worshipping of a leader.

c) Leadership refusing to answer/discuss genuine concerns of members. Any healthy leadership should be willing to discuss any concerns their congregation may have about things happening in the ministry and decisions being made. Of course, the question should be asked respectfully and at an appropriate time and place, but refusing to answer genuine questions or concerns is a red flag.

d) Inappropriate outbursts of anger or shouting at congregants. Any leader who cannot control their temper and is abusive towards the congregation for any reason is a massive warning sign.

e) Threats of ostracising and punishing those who do not conform to the "rules" of the leadership result in fear (2 Timothy 1:7). This one is closely linked to point (b) above regarding the culture of the group but has to do with the treatment of others who dare to question leadership and the negative way they are then treated.

All the above could also be described as control, domination and manipulation, which are characteristics of the spirit of Jezebel. Environments with these characteristics are very unhealthy and ungodly for an individual to be in and will have a detrimental effect on a person's spiritual well-being.

4. Confidential information shared openly

One of the things we should expect to see in godly leadership is the correct and decent way that they treat other people, whether in their absence or presence. Where leaders feel the need to inappropriately berate members during public meetings or disclose personal confidential information previously shared privately with leaders as gossip is quite telling: *And besides they learn to be idle, wandering about from house to house, and not only idle but* *also gossips and busybodies, saying things which they ought not (***1 Timothy 5:13**; *NKJV).*

Gossip is "Conversations about personal details about other people's lives, whether rumour or fact, especially when malicious", and when done in a setting for the hearing of others with whom it does not concern. Leadership that wilfully shares others' private information for the sake of turning others against them is ungodly.

Slander is a partially true or totally false and malicious statement that damages somebody's reputation. Unfortunately, gossip and slander have become "acceptable" in some circles. They are no longer treated as sin and are often promoted by false leadership to promote their agenda and maintain ungodly control by instilling fear in others. Does the leadership sin in this way or encourage you to sin by partaking in theirs?

There are situations where it may become necessary to divulge personal information in line with biblical protocol and procedure to encourage a person to turn away from the error of their ways:

> *"Moreover, if your brother sins against you, go and tell him his fault between you and him alone. If he hears you, you have gained your brother. But if he will not hear, take with you one or two more, that 'by the mouth of two or three witnesses every word may be established.' And if he refuses to hear them, tell it to the church. But if he refuses even to hear the church, let him be to you like a heathen and a tax collector (***Matthew 18:15-17**; *NKJV).*

This scripture is about resolving conflicts in the Church, not a license to reject those the leadership may perceive as a "problem". A person should be approached privately and later with a few witnesses if the first attempt does not work. Later, it should involve only those people to whom it is relevant within the local church family. Obviously, there are times when an issue is so serious that an individual may be disciplined and ejected from the fellowship, but these are usually rare occasions. Every effort should be made to restore that person privately first, and biblical protocol should always be followed. Whatever has occurred, God NEVER sanctions gossip and slander. They are both sins.

5. Ungodly Treatment of ex-members

Here are a few questions to contemplate about the treatment of members that have left the group for whatever reason:

1. Are those inside the group expected to treat others differently simply because they have left?

2. Can healthy friends and family relationships be maintained even though a person decides to move on?

3. Are former members alienated because the leadership considers them a "problem"?

The Bible clearly tells us we should love each other and that this love for one another is evidence of our relationship with Christ. *A new commandment I give to you, that you love one another; as I have loved you, that you also love one another. By this all will know that you are My disciples if you have love for one another"* (**John 13:34-35**; *NKJV).*

How your church or organisation encourages you to treat other believers who have moved on is very telling. If you are encouraged to believe that someone is no longer saved because they worship somewhere else, ask yourself, "Is this a godly attitude towards my brothers and sisters in Christ"? God has many parts of the vineyard for His people, and sometimes, people may move to a different ministry for legitimate and healthy reasons. However, in some extreme cases, the leadership blatantly encourages people to cut off those who leave and have nothing whatsoever to do with them, simply because the leadership says so.

Unless a person is wilfully living in unrepentant gross sin and no longer attempting to live the Christian life, there is no biblical reason to cut someone off because they no longer worship within your group. This is another form of control.

6. Minimising - implying God "overlooks" sin

Sin is always wrong in God's eyes, and He has made it clear in His Word what kinds of things are unacceptable. The Book of Hebrews says *Jesus Christ is the same yesterday, today, and forever* (**Hebrews 13:8**; NKJV). Any attempt to give the impression that God will allow certain sins when the Bible says otherwise is a massive red flag. Minimising the seriousness of sin generally is usually an indicator that things are being hidden and could be a breeding ground for other issues, such as:

- Covering sin in the leadership and punishing those who complain about them.
- Leadership refusing to report criminal matters to the appropriate authorities.

A leader who believes God will overlook their sins because of all their "hard work for God" or "sacrifices they have made" is totally deluded. Sin is always offensive to God, and His standards do not change according to the "anointing" or "gifting" of an individual.

Some leaders will go as far as to convince unsuspecting congregants, usually in the privacy of their office when they are alone, that God does not mind them having sexual treats as a reward for their "great sacrifices" to the work of God. They may even convince their victims that they are privileged to perform such an "honoured" role in the Kingdom. Nothing could be further from the truth; the leader and their victim are being seriously deceived if this happens. This is just one example, but it may manifest in other equally damaging ways, such as inappropriately using church funds or lying to the congregation about church matters as if they were of no consequence and God did not notice.

7.   Being discouraged from personally hearing God

Does everything have to be filtered through a leader? Are you made to feel that you cannot properly hear from God for yourself? Is anything you share with the leadership dismissed as if God could not be talking to you personally?

The scriptures tell us that all believers can hear God for themselves, and it is not just some special privilege for certain people: "*My sheep hear My voice, and I know them, and they follow Me*" (**John 10:27**; NKJV). God knows how to speak to individuals, but if you are not being encouraged to hear God for yourself, you will always be vulnerable to the dictates of others. Yes, some people can indeed be able to tune into God more quickly than others because of gifting and practice. However, if a person is made to feel that they can't tune into God for themselves in any way, shape, or form, they are in a very vulnerable and dangerous position.

8. Redefining sin

The Bible warns against the redefining of sin: *Woe to those who call evil good, and good evil; Who put darkness for light, and light For darkness; Who put bitter for sweet, and sweet for bitter!* (**Isaiah 5:20**; *NKJV).* Examples of common things redefined to control and manipulate others:

- Unavailability to attend a particular meeting is labelled as rebellion.

- Refusing to lie to cover someone's back and being told that God will punish you.

- Being constantly told you have a spirit of pride simply because you do not agree with everything the leadership tells you to.

There are so many situations a person may experience in a church setting that can make them extremely uncomfortable. People should not ignore their gut feelings about a situation but prayerfully ask God for clarity about what to do. An uncomfortable gut feeling may be God's way of gently nudging you not to ignore something. It may well be the Holy Spirit stirring your spirit to be alert and do something about your situation immediately.

9. Loyalty rewards

Corrupt leadership will often reward people for being loyal to them by placing them in positions and giving them titles inappropriately. In most cases, the individual is not really equipped, trained, or even mature enough for the role they are given but feels so honoured that they will happily go along with the leadership plan. There is a constant threat that should they dare to do anything displeasing to the leader, their position becomes untenable and may be taken away at the whim of their leader. The promise of being rewarded in this way is another method of control where a person may be led to believe that they are not quite up to standard yet for the promised position. They will simply try harder to conform to the leader's expected standards but may constantly ultimately fail over something rather minute. If the person does ever attain the promised position, they will constantly be indebted to the leader and demonstrate complete and utter loyalty.

The Apostle Peter gives some insight into what should be expected of leaders:

> The elders who are among you I exhort, I who am a fellow elder and a witness of the sufferings of Christ, and also a partaker of the glory that will be revealed: Shepherd the flock of God which is among you, serving as overseers, not by compulsion but willingly, not for dishonest gain but eagerly; nor as being lords over those entrusted to you, but being examples to the flock (**1 Peter 5:1-3**; NKJV).

The Apostle Paul also warns of the consequences of putting a person in a position of leadership inappropriately:

> He must manage his own family well, having children who respect and obey him. For if a man cannot manage his own household, how can he take care of God's church? A church leader must not be a new believer, because he might become proud, and the devil would cause him to fall. Also, people outside the church must speak well of him so that he will not be disgraced and fall into the devil's trap (**1 Timothy 3:4-7** NLT).

Anyone in a position of authority and power should have the necessary people skills, maturity, and attitude to look after God's people properly and appropriately in line with their position. Their position should be in line with God's calling for their lives, not simply a reward for loyalty. They should never be put into leadership positions to fulfil someone else's agenda. This can cause severe problems as the individual may lack maturity and be used by the leadership to further control, manipulate, and dominate others. Furthermore, it can be quite devastating later down the line when the individual discovers that they were manipulatively put in a position as a reward and simply being used.

10. Failure of leadership to act

Despite the obvious dangers when a leader misbehaves by carrying out certain actions, it is also highly problematic whenever they fail to take the necessary and appropriate action in a situation.

> *Now Eli was very old; and he heard everything his sons did to all Israel, and how they lay with the women who assembled at the door of the tabernacle of meeting. So he said to them, "Why do you do such things? For I hear of your evil dealings from all the people. No, my sons! For it is not a good report that I hear. You make the Lord's people transgress. If one-man sins against another, God will judge him. But if a man sins against the Lord, who will intercede for him?" Nevertheless, they did not heed the voice of their father, because the Lord desired to kill them (**1 Samuel 2:22-25**; NKJV).*

Eli was a senior leader responsible for his subordinates who also had leadership positions. Due to the bad behaviour of Eli's two sons, God desired to kill them, but if their father had addressed the situation earlier, perhaps this could have been avoided. No one is perfect, but a leader is responsible for knowing who they have presiding over other people in their ministry and taking appropriate action where necessary. Not only was God displeased with his sons, but He was also not impressed with Eli's lack of action in disciplining his two sons:

> *Then the Lord said to Samuel: "Behold, I will do something in Israel at which both ears of everyone who hears it will tingle. In that day I will perform against Eli all that I have spoken concerning his house, from beginning to end. For I have told him that I will judge his house forever for the iniquity which he knows, because his sons made themselves vile, and he did not restrain them* (**1 Samuel 3:11-13**; *NKJV*).

Eli was responsible for taking appropriate action when he discovered his sons were involved in wrongdoings but failed to do so. Although he spoke to them concerning their behaviour, he failed to do anything about it. Any leader responsible for others in a position of leadership underneath them has a duty of care to address issues that may arise and deal with the offending parties appropriately and swiftly.

11. Favouritism and misuse

A person may have talents, be gifted, have status, be a large donor, be well educated, have a charismatic personality, have a great testimony, etc., and because of this, they are favoured or used inappropriately. *Then Peter opened* *his mouth and said: "In truth I perceive that God shows no partiality (**Acts 10:34**; NKJV).*

Preferential treatment creates divisions and cliques, causing some to feel less than others. There is nothing wrong with having any of the above, but how are others who don't have such qualities treated? A leader is responsible for the entire flock, not just a select few.

Let me give a few examples: always the same people being asked to lead special projects, lead prayer, give presentations, and sing the lead when others are equally suited. This can cause others to feel inadequate and overlooked. Or a person who is beginning to operate in the gift of prophecy being exalted to a status they are not mature enough to handle and eventually falling. The emphasis was more on the gifts making the ministry look good than on the development of the individual's character. Perhaps it may be someone who has what is regarded as an "amazing story" or "a powerful testimony". Maybe they used to be a prostitute or drug dealer, and God miraculously changed their lives. However, they are prematurely used as a poster person representing the success of the ministry instead of the leadership correctly discerning whether the person was truly ready to deal with any spiritual backlash that may come with a vengeance.

If the leader has wrong motives, there may be a disproportionate emphasis placed on the "greatness" of the organisation/ministry as opposed to the greatness of God, which may lead to:

- Individuals feeling used and abused at the expense of their spiritual wellbeing.
- Others may feel less than if they are always overlooked and disregarded.

- A person becoming puffed up with pride in seeing themselves as better than others.

Summary of warning signs

1. Excessive time in church at the expense of important relationships
2. Pressure to give financially
3. Ungodly treatment of congregants
4. Confidential information shared openly
5. Ungodly treatment of ex-members
6. Minimising—implying that God overlooks sin
7. Discouraged from personally hearing God
8. Redefining sin
9. Loyalty rewards
10. Leadership failure to act
11. Favouritism and misuse

Chapter 4

Twisted Scripture

The term "twisted scripture" refers to the Word of God being misinterpreted and applied to situations in which it does not have any sound biblical relevance. As the Word of God is held in such high esteem and rightly so, a person who does not know what the Word of God says about a particular matter or subject is highly vulnerable to someone else's misinterpretation and ulterior motives. Therefore, it is vital for individuals to know the scriptures for themselves and utilise resources that enable them to rightly divide God's Holy Word.

The Apostle Paul encouraged young Timothy to ensure that he uses the word of God correctly and accurately: *Study and do your best to present yourself to God approved, a workman [tested by trial] who has no reason to be ashamed, accurately handling and skilfully teaching the word of truth* (**2 Timothy 2:15**; *AMP*). Paul also reminds Titus of the doctrinal responsibility of leadership:

> *He must hold firmly to the trustworthy word [of God] as it was taught to him, so that he will be able both to give accurate instruction in sound [reliable, error-free] doctrine and to refute those who contradict [it by explaining their error]* (**Titus 1:9**; *AMP*).

Sound doctrine was extremely important to the Apostle Paul when teaching others as he repeatedly exhorts Timothy to develop the same respect for God's word: *But as for you, teach the things which are in agreement with sound doctrine [which produces men and women of good character whose lifestyle identifies them as true Christians]* (**Titus 2:1**; AMP). Correct teaching of the Word of God has the potential to enable people to develop good character and lifestyles that resemble their relationship with Jesus Christ as their Lord and Saviour. Conversely, the opposite is also true and can cause severe damage to a person's character if they adhere to a faulty interpretation of the scriptures.

A leader may either ignorantly misinterpret the scripture because they do not have the correct understanding or purposely use it to manipulate others for their personal agenda. Either way, a great deal of damage can be done in a person's life if they follow through with the wrong interpretation given to them. Unfortunately, many scriptures have the potential to be misquoted and used out of context to manipulate others. We will look at some common ones that are often used and a few that are not so common.

The following verse is sometimes erroneously used to initiate guilt in a person because they may still be struggling with issues that were in existence before their conversion to Jesus Christ. It may cause a person to become overly reliant on a leader because they feel like a failure.

> *Therefore, from now on, we regard no one according to the flesh. Even though we have known Christ according to the flesh, yet now we know Him thus no longer. Therefore, if anyone is in Christ, he is a new creation; old things have passed away; behold, all things have become new (***2 Corinthians 5:16-17***; NKJV).*

A person may erroneously be led to believe that there is something terribly wrong with them, as they may believe the old thinking patterns or behaviours are still ever-present, yet to pass away. They somehow feel something is wrong with them, or they are stuck. Therefore, this scripture can be used as a battering ram against them instead of a word of encouragement that there has indeed been a change in their lives which will eventually become more evident as time passes by. Let us have a look at this scripture again in the Amplified version:

> So, from now on we regard no one from a human point of view [according to worldly standards and values]. Though we have known Christ from a human point of view, now we no longer know Him in this way. Therefore, if anyone is in Christ [that is, grafted in, joined to Him by faith in Him as Saviour], he is a new creature [reborn and renewed by the Holy Spirit]; the old things [the previous moral and spiritual condition] have passed away. Behold, new things have come [because spiritual awakening brings a new life] (**2 Corinthians 5:16-17**; AMP).

When a person becomes a new creation in Christ, the old things mentioned in the above verse pertain to their previous moral and spiritual conditions. It does not necessarily mean those old behaviours or ways of thinking immediately change. Therefore, a person may feel bad if the person ministering to them does not have a mature understanding of the new life in Christ Jesus and is judgmental of other people's struggles. Although a person can point to a particular time when they got saved, salvation is a continuing journey which we must walk in daily with the help of our loving Heavenly Father. Therefore, when the scripture tells us we must work out our salvation, it is talking about pursuing those things that will personally enable them to mature in Christ, as Paul alludes to in the verse below:

> *So then, my dear ones, just as you have always obeyed [my instructions with enthusiasm], not only in my presence, but now much more in my absence, continue to work out your salvation [that is, cultivate it, bring it to full effect, actively pursue spiritual maturity] with awe-inspired fear and trembling [using serious caution and critical self-evaluation to avoid anything that might offend God or discredit the name of Christ]* (**Philippians 2:12***; AMP).*

The danger of not fully appreciating and understanding what these scriptures are saying is that a person may feel they must commit to close monitoring of every area of their life by a leader as they are so "weak". As a result, they may become overly dependent on a particular person for their spiritual assessment of how they are doing instead of trusting in Christ for their growth. This is not to say we do not need others to support us, but an unnecessarily heavy reliance on another person is unhealthy and could be a red warning flag of potential danger.

Let us consider a very common Old Testament scripture that is often misused and grossly taken out of biblical context to control others: *Saying, "Do not touch My anointed ones, And do My prophets no harm"* (**Psalm 105:15**; NKJV). This verse is God talking about the children of Israel and His faithful protection of them. It is often misused to silence others who may not be happy about what they see in leadership and used as a veiled threat to those who want to challenge them in any way, shape, or form. The fact is that <u>EVERY</u> New Testament believer is the Lord's anointed, not just some special elite of leadership. The word "touch" in the New King James version means "to physically strike or hit or to grab hold of someone". It has absolutely nothing to do with voicing opinions about the genuine concerns of others. The Bible does not tell us to ignore sinful behaviour that comes to light in the life of our leaders.

Some other verses used manipulatively to control others can be found in Numbers chapter twelve:

> *Then Miriam and Aaron spoke Against Moses because of the Ethiopian woman whom he had married; for he had married an Ethiopian woman. So they said, "Has the Lord indeed spoken only through Moses? Has He not spoken through us also?" And the Lord heard it. (Now the man Moses was very humble, more than all men who were on the face of the earth.) Suddenly the Lord said to Moses, Aaron, and Miriam, "Come out, you three, to the tabernacle of meeting!" So, the three came out. Then the Lord came down in the pillar of cloud and stood in the door of the tabernacle and called Aaron and Miriam. And they both went forward. Then He said, "Hear now My words: If there is a prophet among you, I, the Lord, make Myself known to him in a vision; I speak to him in a dream. Not so with My servant Moses; He is faithful in all My house. I speak with him face to face, Even plainly, and not in dark sayings; And he sees the form of the Lord. Why then were you not afraid To speak against My servant*

*Moses?" So, the anger of the Lord was aroused against them, and He departed. And When the cloud departed from above the tabernacle, suddenly Miriam became leprous, as white as snow. Then Aaron turned toward Miriam, and there she was, a leper. So Aaron said to Moses, "Oh, my lord! Please do not lay this sin on us, in which we have done foolishly and in which we have sinned (**Numbers 12:1-11***; NKJV).*

These scriptures are commonly used to frighten people against saying anything regarded as "negative" against leadership and keep them in check. Aaron and Miriam were out of order, and punishment from God followed. Moses had not done anything wrong whatsoever, but Miriam and Aaron had become disgruntled and used the excuse of his wife to find fault with him. God does not punish people with legitimate concerns about their leadership. These verses are not a warning about people speaking up about such concerns.

Unscrupulous leaders sometimes use the next verse with persons coming to them for pastoral care and support during difficult times due to sickness or other adverse situations in their lives:

*As long as I am in the world, I am the light of the world. When he had thus spoken, he spat on the ground, and made clay of the spittle, and he anointed the eyes of the blind man with the clay, And said unto him, Go, wash in the pool of Siloam, (which is by interpretation, Sent.) He went his way therefore, and washed, and came seeing (**John 9:5-7***; NKJV).*

Sometimes, it is used as a "proof" text to manipulate someone into accepting things that ordinarily would be perceived as highly inappropriate for them to be "healed". Notice that this unusual method of healing the blind man was done in a public setting with many witnesses. Any leader who wants to perform unusual things on a person for healing or deliverance purposes in private needs to be seriously challenged. God may well prompt someone to do things out of the ordinary, but if it needs to be done in secret with no witnesses that you feel personally comfortable with, beware!

The scriptures that command us not to judge others are often taken out of the correct biblical context. It is usually cited whenever someone highlights wrongdoing within the leadership or the church organisation: *"Judge not, that you be not judged. For with what judgment you judge, you will be judged; and with the measure you use, it will be measured back to you* (**Matthew 7:1-2**; NKJV). However, you will not usually hear this scripture being used to accuse someone of doing something perceived as being right.

Let us look at these verses more closely in the Amplified version:

> *"Do not judge and criticize and condemn [others unfairly with an attitude of self-righteous superiority as though assuming the office of a judge], so that you will not be judged [unfairly]. For just as you [hypocritically] judge others [when you are sinful and unrepentant], so will you be judged; and in accordance with your standard of measure [used to pass out judgment], judgment will be measured to you* (**Matthew 7:1-2**; AMP).

The scriptures are not telling us that we cannot judge a situation or a person's actions, but we should be mindful we are not acting in a superior manner of self-righteousness. We should indeed use wisdom, common sense, ethical courage, and the written word of God to distinguish between right and wrong, morally and doctrinally. There are many judgements that are not only legitimate but are commanded. Furthermore, we must also consider ourselves as it would be hypocritical to pass judgement about something we ourselves are doing in our lives.

So, the Bible is not telling us we cannot judge sinful behaviour in others, especially in our leadership, as it would be very unwise and dangerous not to. The following verses are clearly telling believers that we are commanded to make certain judgements: *Do not judge according to appearance, but judge with righteous judgment"* (**John 7:24**; NKJV), and *For what have I to do with judging those also who are outside? Do you not judge those who are inside?* (**1 Corinthians 5:12**; NKJV). These verses clearly state that there is room to evaluate a situation fairly, but we should not do so superficially and arrogantly. It is the responsibility of those within the Body of Christ to fairly assess the behaviour and attitudes, even if those under scrutiny are in leadership positions. The Apostle John also encourages us to assess what people say:

> *Beloved, do not believe every spirit, but test the spirits, whether they are of God; because many false prophets have gone out into the world. By this you know the Spirit of God: Every spirit that confesses that Jesus Christ has come in the flesh is of God, and every spirit that does not confess that Jesus Christ has come in the flesh is not of God. And this is the spirit of the Antichrist,*

*which you have heard was coming, and is now
already in the world (***1 John 4:1-3***; NKJV).*

The idea behind testing the spirits is to discern the truth and arrive at a conclusion, a judgement. Suppose we were to gullibly accept what someone professes to be simply because of their title or position. In that case, we will place ourselves in real danger by submitting ourselves to their authority and associating with them. The real reason people use the prohibition about "not judging" is because they are trying to hide or cover up something. There is manipulation at work and a desire to control the situation to their advantage or cover up wrongful behaviour. *Can we judge or not? Scripture gives us evidence we can "judge righteously" but we should avoid "passing judgment" (condemning). In a positive sense, "to judge" means to carefully assess a situation and come to a right conclusion* (Chrnalogar, 2000:64).

A common accusation often thrown at people is "you need to forgive". It usually comes after some wrong has been done to a person and it has never been properly addressed. The person who has been wronged will be accused of being unforgiving or bitter if they try to address the wrong perpetrated against them. Verses like the following are often used as a weapon against such a person: *Then Peter came to Him and said, "Lord, how often shall my brother sin against me, and I forgive him? Up to seven times?"* (**Matthew 18:21-22**; NKJV). The idea is that the person wronged should just forget and move on with a "forgiving heart", regardless of whether the situation has been properly addressed or not.

In the same chapter of Matthew, Jesus tells a parable about an unforgiving servant who owed a massive debt to a King. When he is unable to satisfy the debt, he begs for time to pay and promises to pay in full. The King, however, forgives him the entire debt, but when the same servant sees someone that owes him a comparatively smaller amount than what he had just been forgiven, he grabs him by the throat and commands the debt owed to him to be fully paid immediately. Although the man promises to pay in time, the servant refuses to have mercy and throws him into prison, and the unfair situation is relayed to the King.

> *Then his master, after he had called him, said to him, 'You wicked servant! I forgave you all that debt because you begged me. Should you not also have had compassion on your fellow servant, just as I had pity on you?' And his master was angry and delivered him to the torturers until he should pay all that was due to him. "So My heavenly Father also will do to you if each of you, from his heart, does not forgive his brother his trespasses" (**Matthew 18:32-34***; NKJV*).

This scripture is used inappropriately to persuade a person to let go of a matter, lest God severely punish them. Indeed, the Bible commands us to forgive, and I have dedicated a whole chapter on forgiveness later in this book. Still, these verses are often twisted out of context as it does not tell us to ignore wrongdoing and is certainly not telling someone to allow themselves to be mistreated or abused in some way. Instead, it is an encouragement to show the same compassion and forgiveness we have experienced from God when we repent towards others.

Johnson and Van Vonderen in their book about spiritual abuse say, "*...it is possible to both forgive someone and still stay away from them. It does not necessarily mean you are going to trust them or have a close relationship with them again*"

(Johnson et al. 1991:102). I would even go as far as saying you can forgive someone yet report their criminal behaviour to the police and testify against them in court. Forgiveness does not negate issues being adequately addressed nor cover them up and brush them aside.

The next few verses have been used by those in leadership positions to convince a person coming to them for ministry to submit to highly inappropriate touching for the sake of healing or deliverance from demonic spirits.

> *When Elisha came into the house, there was the child, lying dead on his bed. He went in therefore, shut the door behind the two of them, and prayed to the Lord. And he went up and lay on the child, and put his mouth on his mouth, his eyes on his eyes, and his hands on his hands; and he stretched himself out on the child, and the flesh of the child became warm. He returned and walked back and forth in the house, and again went up and stretched himself out on him; then the child sneezed seven times, and the child opened his eyes"* **(2 Kings 4:32-35**; *NKJV).*

This scripture above can be twisted and taken totally out of context to break down a person's defences to intimate, inappropriate body-to-body contact for supposed healing and deliverance from the "spirit of death". It can also be used as an excuse to become intimate as a way of "transferring the anointing". Let's be very clear: God would <u>NEVER</u> expect anyone to compromise themselves and indulge in sinful behaviour to be healed, delivered, receive spiritual gifts, or for anointing. The prophet Elisha was used in this way specifically to raise the child in those days, which was in a different dispensation from us in the New Testament church today. This story in the Bible was in the Old Testament before the outpouring of the Holy Spirit, and has absolutely nothing to do with how God chooses to operate today.

These scenarios may seem extreme to some and hard to imagine. Still, it was a scripture used in the Jim Jones mass suicide/murder in Guyana in 1978, where over nine hundred people died under the guise of following the leader and obeying "God's will". Another sad event was David Koresh and the Davidians in Waco, Texas, 1993. The leader's twisted interpretation of scripture resulted in seventy-six people's death. Interestingly, in both tragedies, the followers believed their leader was directly hearing from God. This was even though the same leader sexually abused some at the time. The leader's twisting of the scriptures convinced the followers that what they were doing was sanctioned by God. In both instances, according to survivors of both tragedies and witnesses who had managed to escape beforehand, many people felt uncomfortable. They were made to feel as if they were being rebellious. The leaders even convinced other followers to turn against anyone that voiced concerns or wanted to leave.

Twisting and manipulating the scripture is not a new phenomenon but something repeated over the centuries. The black holocaust of colonial slavery was a significant time in history when Bible scriptures were misinterpreted to subdue slaves that had been kidnapped from the African continent. The scriptures were 'interpreted' for them and used to keep slaves under control, convincing them that God had ordained them to serve their 'superior masters' whilst justifying the slave master's barbaric treatment of them through the supposed endorsement of the scripture.

*Slaves, obey your earthly masters in everything; and do it, not only when their eye is on you and to curry their favour, but with sincerity of heart and reverence for the Lord. Whatever you do, work at it with all your heart, as working for the Lord, not for human masters (***Colossians 3:22-23***; NIV).*

*Slaves, in reverent fear of God submit yourselves to your masters, not only to those who are good and considerate, but also to those who are harsh. For it is commendable if someone bears up under the pain of unjust suffering because they are conscious of God. But how is it to your credit if you receive a beating for doing wrong and endure it? But if you suffer for doing good and you endure it, this is commendable before God (***1 Peter 2:18-20***; NIV).*

Slave masters usually considered themselves Christians and would point to such scriptures to bolster their position that God endorses slavery. Many scholars have written about this intentional misuse of the scriptures during this period in history to endorse a form of slavery that had absolutely no resemblance to the slavery written about in the pages of the Bible.

Slavery in the biblical Hebrew community in no ways even remotely resembled slavery in America. Slavery among the biblical Hebrews was more akin to indentured servitude. This kind of slavery involved a legal contract wherein both parties agree to terms of a master-slave arrangement. The master slave contractual agreement was invoked under extreme conditions, and it never had anything to do with race. Neither did it have anything to with creating a permanent underclass. And the Hebrews definitely did not intend to build their entire economy on slavery like the American slavery system (Williams, 2018:132).

Slavery during Hebrew times resembled a form of a contractual agreement between two parties, usually for a limited time. For example, if someone had entered such an agreement to pay off a debt that they owed. There were laws in the scriptures about how slaves should be treated by their masters, as well as a six-year limit for a time in which they should serve, "*If a man beats his male or female slave with a club and the slave dies as a result, the owner must be punished* (**Exodus 21:20**; NLT).

> "*If a man hits his male or female slave in the eye and the eye is blinded, he must let the slave go free to compensate for the eye. And if a man knocks out the tooth of his male or female slave, he must let the slave go free to compensate for the tooth* (**Exodus 21:26-27**; NLT).

> Also, in the same chapter of Exodus, it reads, "*Kidnappers must be put to death, whether they are caught in possession of their victims or have already sold them as slaves* (**Exodus 21:16**; NLT). *The Bible does not endorse slavery as it was practised in America. Through misinterpretation and misapplication of the Bible, it became a powerful weapon used against the slaves. Because an evil system*

> manipulated the historical Jesus and the
> Christian faith by using them for its nefarious
> purposes, it does not mean that the living
> Christ conspired with slaveholders. On the
> contrary, it was the theology of Jesus that
> empowered many of the slave rebellions and
> uprisings (Williams, 2018:134).

Whilst many misinterpreted the Bible to suit their own agenda in kidnapping, keeping and brutalising slaves, others reading the same Bible were inspired by its teachings and their relationship with Jesus Christ to stand up to the evil institution of slavery. People such as Nat Turner, Harriet Tubman, and Frederick Douglas, to name a few. Frederick Douglas, who was born into slavery, eventually escaped to freedom.

> Although the institution of slavery sought
> to use Jesus Christ and the Bible to keep
> slaves "in their place," Douglas saw through
> the religious hypocrisy and made a clear
> distinction between the "Christianity of
> Christ" and the "Christianity of America." He
> challenged Christian slaveholders and the
> clergy who endorsed slavery to repent, lest
> they remain hopelessly stuck in the throes
> of religious hypocrisy and at odds with God
> (Williams, 2018:135).

The twisting of scriptures to endorse and uphold slavery is probably one of the greatest examples of the gross misinterpretation of the Bible. Unfortunately, we still see the fruits of this misinterpretation in our world today regarding some of the racist ideologies birthed and solidified during those times. These ideologies have undoubtedly had far-reaching effects on the descendants of African slaves worldwide.

It is very easy to cherry-pick scriptures to support a particular narrative whilst ignoring others that are in total contrast to a particular behaviour or way of thinking. The consequences of this are potentially quite devastating for an individual or group of individuals being hurt because of it. Therefore, we must get to know scriptures for ourselves and discern with the help of the Holy Spirit what is happening in any given situation.

Chapter 5

Sexual Exploitation by leaders

Sexual exploitation by leaders is a grave issue. It has far-reaching consequences for those who have been the victims of such abuse and for the church organisation or group if it is not dealt with appropriately. Whilst some may struggle to believe such things happen, there is enough evidence to the contrary that it happens far more often than many would like to admit. There is often a great deal of confusion about this issue and how best to handle it. So, I will look at this issue from three different perspectives.

1. How did God deal with sexual exploitation by leaders in the Bible?
2. How do professional organisations view sexual interactions between a professional and a client?
3. How should the Church handle such situations?

First, let's remind ourselves of our definition of spiritual abuse by leaders given at the beginning of this book:

> *When members of the clergy or anyone in a leadership role control, dominate or manipulate others at the expense of their spiritual well-being. Within this context, it would be appropriate to include Sunday school teachers, House group leaders, choir*

> directors, department heads, or anyone within
> a recognised leadership role.

We will start with a very well-known character, King David. Now, David was a king who was genuinely called and appointed by God to replace the previous King Saul, who had been disobedient.

The Bible says,

> *"But now your kingdom shall not continue. The Lord has sought for Himself a man after His own heart, and the Lord has commanded him to be commander over His people, because you have not kept what the Lord commanded you"* (**1 Samuel 13:14***; NKJV*).

> *This scripture is directed at King Saul, telling him God has chosen to replace him with a man after his own heart. David was a man of war, and God had enabled him to win many battles, which everyone in his time was fully aware of: So, the women sang as they danced, and said: "Saul has slain his thousands, And David his ten thousands" (***1 Samuel 18:7***; NKJV).*

Here we have a man who was:

1. Chosen and appointed by God,
2. Loved by the people so much so that they sang songs about his military prowess.

David did many great things for God and the people he led, but later in his life, he made a big mistake which would have far-reaching effects on future generations.

*It happened in the spring of the year, at the time when kings go out to battle, that David sent Joab and his servants with him, and all Israel; and they destroyed the people of Ammon and besieged Rabbah. But David remained at Jerusalem. Then it happened one evening that David arose from his bed and walked on the roof of the king's house. And from the roof he saw a woman bathing, and the woman was very beautiful to behold. So David sent and inquired about the woman. And someone said, "Is this not Bathsheba, the daughter of Eliam, the wife of Uriah the Hittite?" Then David sent messengers, and took her; and she came to him, and he lay with her, for she was cleansed from her impurity; and she returned to her house. And the woman conceived; so, she sent and told David, and said, "I am with child" (***2 Samuel 11:1-5***; *NKJV*)*.

So far, what this story tells us is:

1. David was out of place: he stayed in Jerusalem at a time when kings normally went to war. This was his first mistake.

2. When he first noticed the woman bathing, he looked for too long, which inflamed lust in his heart.

3. He knew once he enquired that she was a married woman and was, therefore, totally off limits.

4. He planned to sleep with her and did so—it was calculated. This was no slip-up or a mistake; David knew what he was doing.

Sometimes, a leader may be deceived into believing that because God is using them greatly, He will overlook their sin. Maybe they feel entitled to sin as a "treat" for all their sacrifices and hard work, but this is simply a deception, and more than likely, demonically influenced. Or they simply do not understand their position as a leader and the responsibility that comes with it—they are too immature for the role they occupy.

Let's continue examining the story about David and Bathsheba. David sends for the woman's husband and pretends he is enquiring how things are going on the battlefield. He encourages the man to go home and sends gifts to his house, hoping that he will sleep with his wife; therefore, the child could be passed off as his. However, due to the man's integrity, he does not go home and explains why to David in the following verses:

> *And Uriah said to David, "The ark and Israel and Judah are dwelling in tents, and my lord Joab and the servants of my lord are encamped in the open fields. Shall I then go to my house to eat and drink, and to lie with my wife? As you live, and as your soul lives, I will not do this thing"* (**2 Samuel 11:11**; *NKJV*).

David's plan is therefore ruined, and he decides to take further deceptive action to cover up his sin:

> *In the morning it happened that David wrote a letter to Joab and sent it by the hand of Uriah. And he wrote in the letter, saying, "Set Uriah in the forefront of the hottest battle, and retreat from him, that he may be struck down and die." So it was, while Joab besieged the*

> *city, that he assigned Uriah to a place where*
> *he knew there were valiant men. Then the men*
> *of the city came out and fought with Joab. And*
> *some of the people of the servants of David*
> *fell; and Uriah the Hittite died also (***2 Samuel***
> ***11:14-17****; NKJV).*

David, although anointed by God and loved by the people, uses his power and influence to satisfy his selfish desires and have an innocent man killed. Often, a person will look upon a leader as being totally infallible and incapable of doing anything wrong. This causes them to let their guard down, making them more vulnerable. Although God genuinely called David a man after God's own heart, he had weaknesses that he never addressed, and this was his downfall.

> *When the wife of Uriah heard that Uriah*
> *her husband was dead, she mourned for her*
> *husband. And when her mourning was over,*
> *David sent and brought her to his house, and*
> *she became his wife and bore him a son. But*
> *the thing that David had done displeased the*
> *Lord (***2 Samuel 11:26-27***; NKJV).*

What have we established so far:

1. King David was a genuine leader chosen by God.
2. He abused his position and committed sin.
3. He arranged the death of an innocent person to hide his wrongdoing.
4. God saw the whole thing and was displeased.

God then sends the prophet Nathan to confront the King about his actions:

Then the Lord sent Nathan to David. And he came to him and said to him: "There were two men in one city, one rich and the other poor. The rich man had exceedingly many flocks and herds. But the poor man had nothing, except one little ewe lamb which he had bought and nourished; and it grew up together with him and with his children. It ate of his own food and drank from his own cup and lay in his bosom; and it was like a daughter to him. And a traveller came to the rich man, who refused to take from his own flock and from his own herd to prepare one for the wayfaring man who had come to him; but he took the poor man's lamb and prepared it for the man who had come to him." So David's anger was greatly aroused against the man, and he said to Nathan, "As the Lord lives, the man who has done this shall surely die! And he shall restore fourfold for the lamb, because he did this thing and because he had no pity" (**2 Samuel 12:1-6**; *NKJV*).

David is completely oblivious to the parallels between what he had done and the man in the parable. He is so consumed with his desire to hide what he has done that his conscience does not even prick him in the slightest. A leader can still be in the position of leadership yet still struggle with issues whilst trying to hide them to keep up appearances. Let's look at the glaring parallels between what David had done and the parable spoken by the prophet.

1. One man was rich, and the other man was poor; David was a wealthy leader, and Uriah was a simple soldier.

2. The rich man had many flocks and herds, whilst the poor man just had one female lamb he cherished; David had many wives, and Uriah had just one.

3. The rich man refuses to take from his own flock but rather takes the poor man's one and only lamb. Instead of being satisfied with his wives, David takes the only wife of Uriah and sleeps with her.

In his hypocrisy, he becomes angry at the rich man for taking what belonged to the poor man until Nathan exposes him fully:

> *Thus says the Lord: 'Behold, I will raise up adversity against you from your own house; and I will take your wives before your eyes and give them to your neighbour, and he shall lie with your wives in the sight of this sun. For you did it secretly, but I will do this thing before all Israel, before the sun.'" So David said to Nathan, "I have sinned against the Lord." And Nathan said to David, "The Lord also has put away your sin; you shall not die. However, because by this deed you Have given great occasion to the enemies of the Lord to blaspheme, the child also who is born to you shall surely die"* **(2 Samuel 12:11-14**; *NKJV).*

David had abused his position, committed murder, and stolen another man's wife, and there were to be dire consequences for his actions. So, what can we conclude from this story?

- If David had dealt with the lust in his heart for another man's wife, he could have avoided the ensuing dire consequences.

- God blames David for taking another man's wife and does not mention Bathsheba's role except for her being taken—in other words, she was a victim.

- David used his position to sexually exploit Bathsheba, even though she may have believed it was consensual. God saw it differently because of who David was.

- Bathsheba also suffered because she lost her child, but God never ascribed it to her as a punishment, only to David.

- We established through the scriptures that although Bathsheba was an adult, God held King David totally responsible for his sexual interaction with a married woman.

Leaders have a higher level of expectation and accountability in their dealings with those they are presiding over. How do we know this? By looking at what the law required at that time and how God dealt with it. The law demands in the Old Testament that the act of adultery is punishable by death for both parties: *'The man who commits adultery with another man's wife, he who commits adultery with his neighbour's wife, the adulterer, and the adulteress, shall surely be put to death'* (**Leviticus 20:10**; *NKJV*).

The law required that both parties be put to death for the act of adultery. The law was very clear, but in the story of Bathsheba and David, God never once calls what happened between the two of them adultery:

> *Why have you despised the commandment of the Lord, to do evil in His sight? You have killed Uriah the Hittite with the sword; you have taken his wife to be your wife and have killed him with the sword of the people of Ammon* (**2 Samuel 12:9**; *NKJV*).

Thus says the Lord: 'Behold, I will raise up adversity against you from your own house; and I will take your wives before your eyes and give them to your neighbour, and he shall lie with your wives in the sight of this sun. For you did it secretly, but I will do this thing before all Israel, before the sun' (**2 Samuel 12:11-12**; *NKJV*).

Not once in any of the conversations with the prophet Samuel is there any mention of punishment being given out to Bathsheba. He specifically mentions in verse 12 of 2 Samuel 12 that David did it secretly, but as his punishment, his neighbour will sleep with his wives openly. We must be cautious when we encounter situations where a leader becomes involved sexually with a person they are not married to. We cannot make superficial judgements based on how things seem on the surface but need to see things from God's perspective. If this kind of thing happened nowadays, the chances are people would erroneously blame Bathsheba and accuse her of seducing the leader whilst portraying the leader as having "slipped" in a moment of weakness. This merely undermines the enormity and seriousness of what the leader has done and minimises the damaging effects on the congregant they had a responsibility to look after.

The danger of this is we would be guilty of making a judgement based on an unscriptural basis. Even if a woman threw herself at a leader butt naked and pleaded that he should sleep with her, the leader should do what Joseph did (**Genesis 39:11-13**) and run for his life. The leader's role endows them with a higher level of responsibility in such situations, and their "weaknesses" are not an excuse for not doing the right thing.

A leader is always responsible for taking charge in a situation and dealing with it appropriately and swiftly. There is never a situation in which a leader should find themselves that would lead to sexual interaction with a congregant or church member they are not married to. If they feel tempted, it needs to be shared with an appropriate, mature person. Any scenarios that could facilitate such inappropriate interactions should be avoided at all costs.

Now, we will look at another story where people in leadership positions are sexually inappropriate with others:

> *Now the sons of Eli were scoundrels who had no respect for the Lord. or for their duties as priests. Whenever anyone offered a sacrifice, Eli's sons would send over a servant with a three-pronged fork. While the meat of the sacrificed animal was still boiling, the servant would stick the fork into the pot and demand that whatever it brought up be given to Eli's sons. All the Israelites who came to worship at Shiloh were treated this way. Sometimes the servant would come even before the animal's fat had been burned on the altar. He would demand raw meat before it had been boiled so that it could be used for roasting. The man offering the sacrifice might reply, "Take as much as you want, but the fat must be burned first." Then The servant would demand, "No, give it to me now, or I'll take it by force." So, the sin of these young men was very serious in the Lord's sight, for they treated the Lord's offerings with contempt (**1 Samuel 2:12-17; NLT**).*

The sons of Eli were officiating priests in the tabernacle, but they had absolute disregard for the things of God and did exactly as they pleased. Let's continue with the story and see how their father, being their senior leader, deals with the situation:

> Now Eli was very old, but he was aware of what his sons were doing to the people of Israel. He knew, for instance, that his sons were seducing the young women who assisted at the entrance of the Tabernacle. Eli said to them, "I have been hearing reports from all the people about the wicked things you are doing. Why do you keep sinning? You must stop, my sons! The reports I hear among the Lord's people are not good. If someone sins against another person, God can mediate for the guilty party. But if someone sins against the Lord, who can intercede?" But Eli's sons wouldn't listen to their father, for the Lord was already planning to put them to death (**1 Samuel 2:22-25**; *NLT*).

These verses highlight a few things:

1. Eli's sons were priests in the tabernacle.
2. They had no respect for the things of God and treated others with utter contempt.
3. They were having sex with the women serving at the gate of the tabernacle.
4. Others were aware and complained to Eli about his sons' behaviours.
5. They refused to pay any attention to their father's warnings.

They failed to recognise the responsibility of their role and clearly did not understand nor care about the boundaries put in place. God was extremely displeased with how Eli handled the situation and warned him that judgement was about to be enacted against his family:

> Then the Lord said to Samuel, "I am about to do a shocking thing in Israel. I am going to carry out all my threats against Eli and his family, from beginning to end. I have warned him that judgment is coming upon his family forever, because his sons are blaspheming God and he hasn't disciplined them. So I have vowed that the sins of Eli and his sons will never be forgiven by sacrifices or offerings" (**1 Samuel 3:11-14**; NLT).

Key points:

- Eli's sons had leadership roles as priests in the temple, and Eli, a judge of Israel, had authority over them.
- Eli spoke to them and emphasised that what they were doing was a sin against God, but he failed to take appropriate action.
- Eli was judged for his failure in his role as a senior leader, and God pronounced a curse on his family.

It wasn't long before the curse pronounced in chapter three came to pass in the next chapter. The Philistine army defeats Israel, the ark of God is captured, and Eli's sons are killed:

> "Israel has been defeated by the Philistines," the messenger replied. "The people have been

*slaughtered, and your two sons, Hophni and Phinehas, were also killed. And the Ark of God has been captured." When the messenger mentioned what had happened to the Ark of God, Eli fell backward from his seat beside the gate. He broke his neck and died, for he was old and overweight. He had been Israel's judge for forty years (***1 Samuel 4:17-18***; NLT).*

What can we learn from this story?

- A senior leader is responsible for subordinate leaders, and God expects them to address issues swiftly and appropriately.

- People are made vulnerable because of a leader's lack of appropriate action.

God is highly displeased when a leader takes sexual advantage of someone under their pastoral care. David was a King; Eli was a judge, and Eli's sons were priests. As leaders with responsible positions, they were ultimately responsible for their interactions with others. The women in both stories were adults, and even though they may have viewed themselves as "willing" participants, God's responses in both scenarios are quite telling. In King David's case, Bathsheba is not addressed in any way. In Eli's son's case, there is no mention of any punishment for the women at the temple gate.

God views a person involved in sexual sin with a leader differently to sexual sin between two individuals on the same level. There was a significant difference in role and responsibility between a king, priest, or judge and the women. There is a considerable power imbalance between a leader and a congregant. Therefore, it is sexual abuse, and

God will punish the abuser. However, this does, unfortunately, mean that the victim may often also suffer consequences.

Conclusions

- Leaders are always responsible for their interactions with those they lead, counsel, pray for, teach, disciple, etc.

- Even if a person is determined to commit sexual sin with a leader, the leader is still ultimately responsible for putting an immediate stop to it and informing another trusted person immediately.

- Leaders should do their best to avoid vulnerable situations or potential accusations and always have a third-party present in precarious situations.

A leader operates in their role as the expert because of their position, giving advice, counsel, training, direction, or support. They are therefore 100% responsible for all their interactions with anybody coming to them in that capacity. Whatever their leadership role is within a church context, they are ultimately accountable for their behaviour and responses to other people's behaviour towards them.

Chapter 6

Dealing with sexual exploitation

We will now look at dealing with sexual exploitation by leaders and examine some research findings on the clergy sexual abuse of adults before considering how churches should handle such situations appropriately.

Research on clergy sexual abuse of adults

In 2008, Baylor University received a two hundred-thousand-dollar grant from the Ford Foundation to conduct the first national research on clergy sexual abuse of adults. The data for the research was gathered between 2008-2009. The research was based on the growing number of congregants becoming sexually involved with clergies they were not married to, and it was recognised as a serious problem. According to the late Professor Diana Garland of Baylor's School of Social Work, the goals of the research project were:

- to determine the prevalence of clergy sexual abuse of adults.
- to teach religious leaders, congregants, and the general public that sexual activity between a religious leader and a congregant cannot be considered consensual.

- to communicate to survivors and their families that they are not alone and deserve support and professional care.

All the information I will quote from their research can be found at: [www.adultsabusedbyclergy.org, 10th June 2022].

Let me read for you some findings from their report that have been published on their website, "Adults abused by clergy" under the page heading "psychological impacts":

> Consent to sexual relations is not possible due to the power differential between clergy and congregant". It goes on to say, "Sexual violation by a therapist, doctor, or clergy member is not about sex; it is an abuse of power, authority, and trust inherent in the relationship.

Professor Diana Garland also says on the site: "*Many people, including the victims themselves, often label incidences of Clergy Sexual Misconduct with adults as 'affairs'. In reality, they are an abuse of spiritual power by the religious leader.*"

Contrary to what many people think, most victims of sexual abuse by clergy are not children but adult females. This is because incidences of sexual misconduct against adults are not recognised as abuse. The research highlighted that: "*Although clergy of any denomination can sexually exploit children, teens, men, or women, many experts estimate that over 95% of victims of sexual exploitation by clergy are adult women*".

The research also found:

> "Adult victims of sexual exploitation by clergy often don't see themselves as victims. Without wider public awareness of the extent and

*impacts of this form of sexual violence, adults
who have been sexually victimized by a beloved
priest, pastor, minister, rabbi, or other clergy
will remain the "silent majority" of clergy
sexual abuse victims, suffering in their shame
and self-isolation".*

This research in no way undermines the seriousness
of sexual abuse committed against children and teenagers.
However, it highlights a significant misunderstanding, as
adults do not see themselves as victims, nor do other adults
view these adults as victims. The concept of an adult abused
by clergy may be difficult for many to understand. However,
viewing things from a scriptural perspective will bring
tremendous clarity and great healing to the Body of Christ.

Other professional organisations and the judicial system

Many other organisations are very clear about
professional boundaries and responsibilities. They recognise
a power imbalance between the professional and the person
coming to them for help. However, in professions like a
doctor, counsellor, teacher, solicitor, social worker, or dentist,
they would be struck off and possibly imprisoned if they
were to abuse their positions and cross sexual boundaries.
They would be prohibited from practising again, and in
some cases, could be placed on a sexual offender's register
regardless of whether the victim was an adult or not.

How much more so for people who have pastoral
authority and responsibility to God's people? Sadly, the
Church is still struggling to see the enormity of the damage
that leaders inflict on others when they violate their God-given
role in such a way. However, things are changing, and more
and more church organisations have procedures in place to
deal with this grave violation of ministerial boundaries.

Let me highlight one more quote from the adults abused by clergy website,

> *Denominational codes of ethics recognize that mutual consent is not possible in sexual relations between ministers and those they serve. Sexualization of the ministerial relationship is a violation of the sacred boundary between a pastor and members of his or her flock.*

This is a crucial point; sacred boundaries have been crossed whenever a leader of any kind in a Christian context violates their God-given role. Therefore, any such abuse should always be viewed from this biblical perspective.

How should churches handle such situations?

Unfortunately, in many churches today, where a leader is involved in sexual misconduct with another adult, the blame is put on the victim. Often, a victim is re-victimised repeatedly by others in the church who mishandle the situation and are not appropriately trained, experienced, or qualified to handle such weighty matters. The offending leader is usually regarded as having "a slip in a moment of weakness" or "a minor indiscretion".

One of the most heart-breaking statements coming from victims of sexual abuse is that after the sexual abuse, they were "revictimized all over again by the church". The poor and the often abusive way they were treated after mustering up the courage to expose things is quite appalling. They often feel that the church's abusive treatment due to lack of understanding and professional input was more difficult to deal with than the sexual abuse itself. This is possibly one of the main reasons adult victims of sexual abuse do not come forward.

> *Before we get into this question more fully about professional boundaries and the judicial system, let's see what the New Testament says about sexual relationships outside of marriage: But fornication and all uncleanness or covetousness, let it not even be named among you, as is fitting for saints; neither filthiness, nor foolish talking, nor coarse jesting, which are not fitting, but rather giving of thanks* (**Ephesians 5:3-4***; NKJV*).

Let's look a bit deeper into some words used in these passages.

Fornication: illicit sexual relationships and includes adultery and incest.

Fornication: Greek word "porneia" (porniya) – which is where we get our word pornography from.

Derived from the root word "porneuō" (pornua)

Meaning: to prostitute one's body to the lust of another, to give oneself to unlawful sexual intercourse.

In verse 4: *neither filthiness, nor foolish talking, nor coarse jesting, which are not fitting.* This would undoubtedly include lewd conversations of a sexual nature or sexual innuendos, especially with someone who is not your spouse. Let us have a look at those verses in the Amplified version:

> *But sexual immorality and all [moral] impurity [indecent, offensive behaviour] or greed must not even be hinted at among you, as is proper among saints [for as believers our*

> *way of life, whether in public or in private,*
> *reflects the validity of our faith]. Let there be*
> *no filthiness and silly talk, or coarse [obscene*
> *or vulgar] joking, because such things are not*
> *appropriate [for believers]; but instead speak*
> *of your thankfulness [to God]* (**Ephesians**
> **5:3-4**; *AMP).*

The only situation whereby the Bible speaks of sexual intimacy in a favourable way is within the confines of a heterosexual marriage between a man and a woman.

> *Now as to the matters of which you wrote: It*
> *is good (beneficial, advantageous) for a man*
> *not to touch a woman [outside marriage].*
> *But because of [the temptation to participate*
> *in] sexual immorality, let each man have his*
> *own wife, and let each woman have her own*
> *husband* (**1 Corinthians 7:1-2**; *AMP).*

Sexual interaction with anyone other than a spouse of the opposite sex is never acceptable in God's eyes, no matter the circumstances or how "in love" they may be. Any leader interacting in a sexual manner, whether physically, emotionally, or verbally with someone they are not married to, is a grave matter. Sexual innuendos, suggestions, and insinuations in such situations may not have become physical but have already violated boundaries and is equally as serious when things are viewed from a spiritual perspective. The Bible makes it clear that death and life are in the power of the tongue (**Proverbs 18:21**), so even words of a sexual nature can damage another person's soul, especially when the speaker is in the role of a leader.

Fortunately, some countries around the world have very clear guidelines in place to protect congregants from leadership or clergy abuse. For example, in certain states in the USA and Australia, it is a criminal offence for a member of the leadership to engage in any form of sexual activity with a congregant they are not married to, regardless of the congregant's age. But sadly, many other churches worldwide have not had this revelation. Therefore, support for those sexually abused by leadership is seriously lacking.

What should churches do in these situations?

1. Churches need to take the sexual misconduct of their leaders seriously.
2. The abusing leader needs to be held accountable, disciplined, or removed from their leadership position.
3. Appropriate authorities must be contacted immediately, i.e., police or social services.

The issue of getting outside authorities like the police or social services involved is sometimes frowned upon and prohibited by those inside the church group/organisation. As a result, scriptures like this next one are often taken out of context to prevent the crime from being exposed and reported:

> *Dare any of you, having a matter against another, go to law before the unrighteous, and not before the saints? Do you not know that the saints will judge the world? And if the world will be judged by you, are you unworthy to judge the smallest matters? Do you not know that we shall judge angels? How much more,*

things that pertain to this life? (**1 Corinthians 6:1-3**; *NKJV*).

Let's take another look at verse 1 in the Amplified version:

> *Does any one of you, when he has a complaint (civil dispute) with another [believer], are to go to law before unrighteous men (non-believers) instead of [placing the issue] before the saints (God's people)?*

This specifically talks about "civil matters", "small" disputes between neighbours, etc. It is not talking about weightier matters like sexual abuse, sexual harassment by a leader, or anything of that nature.

> *In a civil case, one party is the plaintiff (going to law with a case against his neighbour) and one is the defendant. More than likely, Paul is referring to a fight between Christians over a cow, a piece of property, or a sum of money. He affirms the fact that the ability to decide such matters lies within the body of Christ. Unfortunately, in some places the saints are part of the cover-up (Johnson et al., 1991:103).*

Furthermore, the Bible tells us to obey the laws of the land: *"Let every soul be subject to the governing authorities. For there is no authority except from God, and the authorities that exist are appointed by God"* (**Romans 13:1**; *NKJV*). Another scripture that highlights the importance of obeying the laws in our society is found in **Matthew 22:17-21** (NKJV):

> *Tell us, therefore, what do You think? Is it lawful to pay taxes to Caesar, or not?" But Jesus*

perceived their wickedness, and said, "Why do you test Me, you hypocrites? Show Me the tax money." So, they brought Him a denarius. And He said to them, "Whose image and inscription is this?" They said to Him, "Caesar's." And He said to them, "Render therefore to Caesar the things that are Caesar's, and to God the things that are God's."

Jesus clearly expects us to obey the laws of the land, and if the law says we need to report incidences of sexual misconduct, then we are going against scripture if we disobey. Scripturally, we are only required to disregard any laws that would cause us to disobey God: *"But Peter and the other apostles answered and said: "We ought to obey God rather than men (**Acts 5:29**; NKJV).*

The Bible is certainly not saying that we should keep criminal matters of sexual misconduct and abuse in Church out of the courtroom and deal with things privately inside the Church. The danger with this is that the perpetrator may have been doing such things for some time and getting away with it. Beliefs such as "keep it in the Church" or "keep it quiet so as not to discredit the name of Christ" can potentially put others at risk. So, unless the law tells us to go against scripture, it is scriptural to report crimes of a sexual nature to the appropriate authorities, whether perpetrated against children, teenagers, or adults. Remember, a crime has been committed!

The issue of forgiveness may also be stated as a reason for not reporting a leader to the authorities. Yes, we are required to forgive others, but a person can forgive someone and yet still report them to the police and testify against them in court.

4. Churches need to stop using words like "affair", "consensual", or "complicit".

It is NOT an accurate description of the situation. It is sexual abuse by a leader. Erroneous descriptions minimise the extent of the trauma that the victim experiences and mislead others as to the truth about what has really happened.

5. Churches need to engage professional counsellors or other suitably qualified and experienced persons to support the victim. However, just because someone has a title like minister, pastor, priest, etc., within a church context does not mean they have the necessary ability, skills, or expertise to deal with such weighty matters.

6. Leaders who perpetrate such abuse also need professional help; perhaps deliverance and inner healing may be required.

Why? Because they have sinned against God and have ventured into Satan's domain, thereby spiritually opening a dark door into their own life and quite possibly, the life of their ministry, especially if they are the senior leader. If the perpetrator is a subordinate leader, then not dealing with the situation appropriately also has far-reaching consequences. What the leader does personally or their failure to deal with other leadership issues will have repercussions for the whole ministry, church group or organisation, spiritually and naturally, and this will also have to be dealt with.

So, when it comes to sexual abuse by the leadership, we can summarise this:

1. God views a person involved in sexual immorality with a leader differently from sexual immorality between two individuals on the same level.

2. There is a significant power imbalance between a leader and a congregant; therefore, mutual consent is not possible in sexual relations between those in leadership positions and those they serve.

3. Churches need to stop using words like "affair", "consensual", or "complicit". It is NOT an accurate description of the situation—it is sexual abuse by a leader.

4. Sexual abuse should always be reported to the appropriate authorities immediately, i.e., the police or social services—remember, a crime has been committed!

5. Churches need to engage professional counsellors or other suitably qualified and experienced persons to support the victim.

6. The abusing leader needs to be held fully accountable regardless of the victim's age—they may also need spiritual deliverance and inner healing as they have ventured into the realm of the demonic and are in bondage in this area of their life.

In conclusion

Remember what we have learnt: God does not take it lightly when leaders abuse those they are supposed to be caring for and leading. Sexual abuse is serious in any situation. However, in the context of a church where the perpetrator is the leader or one of the leaders, it can have far-reaching spiritual implications for the victim. It can affect a person's faith, concept of God, mental and emotional well-being, and sometimes an entire ministry, church, or group. It is a weapon that the enemy delights in using against the Body of Christ wherever he has legal rights because of the brokenness and injury in a particular area of a leader's life. The Church needs to have a proper and mature understanding of the spiritual and emotional impact it can have. Therefore, it needs to know how to deal with it appropriately and effectively.

Chapter 7

How Satan attacks the Church

Demons are real, and believers that do not understand this or minimise the existence of our spiritual enemy are at a distinct disadvantage. The Bible mentions spiritual beings in their various forms throughout the scriptures and gives us insight into how they operate and their characteristics. Let us look at a few verses mentioning them: *Be sober, be vigilant; because your adversary the devil walks about like a roaring lion, seeking whom he may devour (**1 Peter 5:8**; NKJV).*

> *For we are not fighting against people made of flesh and blood, but against persons without bodies—the evil rulers of the unseen world, those mighty satanic beings and great evil princes of darkness who rule this world; and against huge numbers of wicked spirits in the spirit world (**Ephesians 6:12**; TLB).*

The Bible gives us insight into the characteristics of evil spirits operating in the life of individuals:

> *When an unclean spirit goes out of a man, he goes through dry places, seeking rest, and finds none. Then he says, 'I will return to my house from which I came.' And when he comes, he finds it empty, swept, and put in order.*

> *Then he goes and takes with him seven other spirits more wicked than himself, and they enter and dwell there; and the last state of that man is worse than the first. So shall it also be with this wicked generation"* (**Matthew 12:43-45**; *NKJV*).

We can see from these verses that demons have personalities and can process information. They are living disembodied spirits with an intense desire to inhabit physical human bodies and cause havoc. Let's have a look at some more verses that show the characteristics of evil spirits:

> *You believe that there is one God. You do well. Even the demons believe and tremble!* (**James 2:19**; *NKJV*).

> *Now there was a man in their synagogue with an unclean spirit. And he cried out, saying, "Let us alone! What have we to do with You, Jesus of Nazareth? Did You come to destroy us? I know who You are the Holy One of God!"* (**Mark 1:23-24**; *NKJV*).

> *When he saw Jesus from afar, he ran and worshiped Him. And he cried out with a loud voice and said, "What have I to do with You, Jesus, Son of the Most High God? I implore You by God that You do not torment me." For He said to him, "Come out of the man, unclean spirit!" Then He asked him, "What is your name?" And he answered, saying, "My name is Legion; for we are many"* (**Mark 5:6-9**; *NKJV*).

Legion was a term used in those times to describe many Roman soldiers, anywhere between three thousand to six thousand men under the control of a governor or a senator. This gives us an insight into the vast number of evil spirits dwelling in the man and that they had a commander and were well organised.

These verses tell us six things about demons:

1. They are persistent
2. They have emotions
3. They are intelligent
4. They are self-aware
5. They can speak
6. They network and communicate with other evil spirits
7. They operate within an organised hierarchy of command

The spiritual realm is very real, but unfortunately, too many Christians ignorantly underestimate the ability of evil spirits, and therefore, are more susceptible to their influences. Just because a person is born again does not mean all the spiritual baggage that existed before their conversion has been dealt with.

A misunderstanding of the following verse can leave the impression that there will be no spiritual problems after a person becomes born again: *Therefore, if anyone is in Christ, he is a new creation; old things have passed away; behold, all things have become new* (**2 Corinthians 5:17**; NKJV). It is only our spirit that becomes born again when a person accepts Jesus Christ as their Lord and Saviour. There will still be things that need to be resolved as we continue with our salvation which is why the scriptures tell us: *Therefore, my beloved, as you have always obeyed, not as in my presence only, but now much more in my absence, work out your own salvation with fear and trembling* (**Philippians 2:12**; NKJV).

Satan hates God, His creation, and especially the Church. Why? Because we are made in God's image, and the only way he can hurt God is by hurting us. God has given us the authority over the powers of darkness and spiritual wickedness through the name of Jesus Christ, but we can only be effective against the enemy's schemes if we understand this. Conversely, believers who know their God and understand the spiritual realm and its principles are a massive threat to Satan and his army.

The early church was very aware of the reality of the spiritual realm, as Jesus delivered many people from evil spirits and commissioned His disciples to do the same. In fact, in the early church, deliverance would often be performed on people before they were baptised, especially if they had been previously involved in things like the occult. This is because they understood the problems that could ensue for a new believer if evil spirits were still inhabiting areas of their lives.

In our 21st century world, there has been a massive rise in people's involvement in the occult, simply because they were either enticed into it by deception or it was passed down through the family bloodline. The word "occult" means "secret" or "mysterious" and comes in many forms, too many to mention in this short book. It is mainly split into two divisions: Divination and Sorcery. The late Derek Prince, in his book, *They Shall Expel Demons*, describes them this way:

> *Divination provides knowledge through supernatural means about people, events, and situations. Frequently it predicts future events.*

> *The contemporary terms for this are fortune-telling, psychic predicting and extrasensory perception (ESP) (Prince, 1998:125).*

> *Sorcery can be considered the twin sister of divination, but this has its own special sphere of activity. It uses various means to make an impact on the physical senses. Some of its tools are drugs, potions, charms, amulets, magic, spells, incantations, and various forms of music (Prince, 1998:130).*

Unfortunately, some of these have found their way into the Church as people seek to "add" or "enhance" their effectiveness in their roles within the Church. However, this is nothing other than a great deception and unwittingly opens demonic doorways into the life of those who dabble in such dark arts.

The following verses in Luke tell us about the ministry of deliverance and healing that was prevalent in Jesus' time:

> *After these things the Lord appointed seventy others also and sent them two by two before His face into every city and place where He Himself was about to go.*

> *Then the seventy returned with joy, saying, "Lord, even the demons are subject to us in Your name." And He said to them, "I saw Satan fall like lightning from heaven. Behold, I give you the authority to trample on serpents and scorpions, and over all the power of the enemy, and nothing shall by any means hurt you* **(Luke 10:1, 17-19;** *NKJV).*

Unfortunately, the Church's lack of spiritual understanding about the warfare we are engaged in has left far too many casualties. The belief that demons cannot affect the life of a born-again believer is a deception that Satan continues to perpetuate. God has given us spiritual authority over the powers of darkness, but we need to enforce that authority.

Satan has many strategies, but some of his best ones are:

- Convincing people that he does not really exist.
- Minimising the extent to which he can influence the life of a born-again believer.

Satan is a legalist, so he and his demons will operate within the confines of their legal, spiritual rights. Sin always gives Satan legal rights, which is why the Bible tells us to deal with sin in its various forms. For example, in the gospel of John, chapter five, Jesus heals a man who had been sick for thirty-eight years. Following the healing, the man could get up and walk by himself. The scripture tells us what happened later in **John 5:14** (AMP): *Afterward, Jesus found him in the temple and said to him, "See, you are well! Stop sinning or something worse may happen to you."*

Open doorways for the demonic are varied and include, but are not limited to:

- Generational sin
- Personal sins
- Corporate sin/Church sin
- Occultic involvement/practices
- Being a victim of sin, someone sinning against us
- Life traumas or accidents

Let's now look at seven ways I have personally seen the enemy gain access to a church or church organisation and negatively affect them. Of course, this list is inconclusive, and there may be others.

1. Sin in the Church family

The Old Testament gives us a good understanding of generational sins and the consequences on descendants:

> And the Lord passed before him and proclaimed, "The Lord, the Lord God, merciful and gracious, longsuffering, and abounding in goodness and truth, keeping mercy for thousands, forgiving iniquity and transgression and sin, by no means clearing the guilty, visiting the iniquity of the fathers upon the children and the children's children to the third and the fourth generation" (**Exodus 34:6-7**; NKJV).

The New Testament Church also understood this principle: *Now as Jesus passed by, He saw a man who was blind from birth. And His disciples asked Him, saying, "Rabbi, who sinned, this man or his parents, that he was born blind?"* (**John 9:1-2**; NKJV).

The disciples understood the principle of the consequences of sin being passed down to children. Therefore, as demons are permitted access into a natural family because of parental sins, they can also gain access to a church family due to the spiritual parents, a ministry, or its leaders.

2. Spirits of sexual lust and perversion

Where a leader is involved in sexual immorality with a congregant, it will form a spiritual soul tie with that person because, from a spiritual perspective, they have become one flesh:

> *Do you not know that your bodies are members of Christ? Shall I then take the members of Christ and make them members of a harlot? Certainly not! Or do you not know that he who is joined to a harlot is one body with her? For "the two," He says, "shall become one flesh"* (**1 Corinthians 6:15-16**; *NKJV*).

In other words, any unclean spirits affecting the leader now have access to spiritually infect the other person, which was initiated through the one-flesh union. However, this spiritual infestation is not limited to penetrative sex but includes many other sexual misconducts, such as fondling, kissing, voyeurism, pornography, etc. Any sexually motivated act or even lustful conversation can open doors of spiritual defilement into a person's life and thereby, the church group or organisation. Let us look at what the Apostle Paul says about how we handle situations where a so-called Christian is unwilling to let go of their immoral lifestyle.

> *But actually, I have written to you not to associate with any so-called [Christian] brother if he is sexually immoral or greedy or is an idolater [devoted to anything that takes the place of God] or is a reviler [who insults or slanders or otherwise verbally abuses others] or is a drunkard or a swindler—you must not so much as eat with such a person. For what business is it of mine to judge outsiders (non-believers)? Do you not judge those who are within the church [to protect the church*

*as the situation requires]? (*1 **Corinthians 5:11-12**; *AMP).*

Paul lists several sins besides sexual immorality that he expects the Corinthian church to deal with for their own protection. Sexual immorality amongst the congregation can open a doorway to the enemy and spread like a virus if not checked and properly addressed by the leadership. It is imperative that sin issues are dealt with and rooted out of a ministry; otherwise, it will spiritually defile and weaken the whole church.

3. Deceiving spirits

The scripture gives us insight into the operation of evil spirits amongst those professing to be in the faith:

> *Now the Spirit expressly says that in latter times some will depart from the faith, giving heed to deceiving spirits and doctrines of demons, speaking lies in hypocrisy, having their own conscience seared with a hot iron, forbidding to marry, and commanding to abstain from foods which God created to be received with thanksgiving by those who believe and know the truth (*1 **Timothy 4:1-3**; *NKJV).*

Any leader that has departed from the faith whilst still operating in their position is being influenced by deceiving spirits and will inevitably promote doctrines of devils. They may still preach, teach, and minister through the laying on of hands but be demonically affected even though they may not be aware. This will have an impact on those who are sitting under their leadership. In verse three above, the mention of *"forbidding to marry, and commanding to abstain from food"* alludes to the fact that there are commandments from people in leadership positions, which is controlling the behaviour of others.

This method of Satan has far-reaching consequences because of the number of people affected by a leader being deceived. A congregant does not have to be aware of a particular sin in a leader's life to be affected by its consequences. They just need to be submitted to their leadership, which is why congregations must continually pray for their leaders.

Evil spirits have absolutely no problem operating in a religious atmosphere, where people are not born again or are more focused on religious rituals and traditions, where the Holy Spirit is not welcomed, or where evil spirits have initiated the teaching. Church leaders and congregants may attend church every Sunday, preach great sermons or sing like a canary, but their hearts are far from God. The scriptures warn us that this will happen in the end times:

> But know this, that in the last days perilous times will come: For men will be lovers of themselves, lovers of money, boasters, proud, blasphemers, disobedient to parents, unthankful, unholy, unloving, unforgiving, slanderers, without self-control, brutal, despisers of good, traitors, headstrong, haughty, lovers of pleasure rather than lovers of God, having a form of godliness but denying its power. And from such people turn away! (**2 Timothy 3:1-5**; NKJV).

The sinful behaviours listed in verses 1–4 are taking place in the lives of those professing to be godly and no doubt in the Church. Although they may, on the surface, appear to be just works of the flesh, each one of them can be a stronghold in a person's life influenced by demonic powers. Due to leadership only having the appearance of godliness on the outside whilst displaying characteristics that are not of God gives an appalling testimony to the Church. This is another ploy of the enemy operating through human weakness to convince others that Christianity is fake, that Christians are hypocrites or other derogatory labels often ascribed to believers.

4.   Spirits of doubt & unbelief in healing

Sickness was never God's plan for us, and as believers, we certainly do not have to accept it. Unfortunately, some churches do not believe in or even preach on God's ability to heal supernaturally right here in the twenty-first century. This seems to be more prevalent in the Western world as opposed to churches in the Southern hemisphere of our world today. If a church does not teach or even believe in healing from sickness and disease, the congregation is more prone to accepting whatever illnesses the devil will throw at them.

The enemy will convince people of lies like:

- God gives sickness as a punishment
- Sickness is a method God uses to teach lessons
- That the premature death of a person was God's will
- Supernatural healing ended with the early church

Healing is a part of the gospel message, and Jesus demonstrated and taught this wherever He went: *Then great multitudes came to Him, having with them the lame, blind, mute, maimed, and many others; and they laid them down at Jesus' feet, and He healed them* (**Matthew 15:30**; *NKJV*).

The Apostles demonstrated miracles, signs, and wonders in the early church:

> Now it came to pass, as Peter went through all parts of the country, that he also came down to the saints who dwelt in Lydda. There he found a certain man named Aeneas, who had been bedridden eight years and was paralyzed. And Peter said to him, "Aeneas, Jesus the Christ heals you. Arise and make your bed." Then he arose immediately. So all who dwelt at Lydda, and Sharon saw him and turned to the Lord (**Acts 9:32-35**; *NKJV*).

Also, the apostle Paul, who never physically met Jesus:

> And it happened that the father of Publius lay sick of a fever and dysentery. Paul went into him and prayed, and he laid his hands on him and healed him. So when this was done, the rest of those on the island who had diseases also came and were healed (**Acts 28:8-9**; *NKJV*).

The early church replicated what Jesus did, and we have the same authority to do likewise. However, the devil has convinced many in the church that healing is not for today or that it only happens in developing countries where people live miles and miles from the nearest hospital. Jesus also encountered similar unbelief in His time:

> But Jesus said to them, "A prophet is not without honour except in his own country, among his own relatives, and in his own house." Now He could do no mighty work there, except that He laid His hands on a few sick people and healed

119

> *them. And He marvelled because of their*
> *unbelief. Then He went about the villages in a*
> *circuit, teaching (**Mark 6:4-6**; NKJV).*

Unbelief is a great hindrance to the healing power of God operating in a ministry. Sadly, God's people sometimes get sick and die prematurely, but the scripture shows us that it does not have to be that way. God has given the Church the authority through Jesus' name to heal the sick right here in the 21st century.

Having said all this, let me clarify that God has given doctors and medical professionals great wisdom, and we should go to the doctors or hospital, especially for serious conditions. I am in no way advocating that people should not seek professional medical advice and treatment.

5.   Spirit of fear

Fear is a major weapon used against the Church: *For God has not given us a spirit of fear, but of power and of love and of a sound mind* (**2 Timothy 1:7**; NKJV). As it shows, fear is a spirit that often works with other demonic spirits to hinder or destroy a ministry.

Example: Not appropriately confronting sin issues because of fear of the people leaving or withholding their financial support can leave open doorways for other spirits to also take up residence in a ministry. This may lead to spirits of compromise, passivity, people pleasing, etc., teaming up with the spirit of fear and tightening the satanic grip on the Church.

> *Just as damaging is the fear of demons due to*
> *lack of understanding of the authority that we*
> *have over them. All too often Christians have*
> *treated demons with superstitious dread, as*

> *if they are in the same category as ghosts or dragons. Corrie ten Boon commented that the fear of demons is from the demons themselves (Prince, 1998:12).*

Fear is very crippling and will stop a person or a ministry in their tracks if they concede to its influence, and the enemy knows this. Therefore, it can be a major hindrance to obeying the direction God has set for our lives, and it will often use seemingly plausible excuses as to why it should be obeyed.

6.   Spirit of idolatry

Churches that overemphasise reverence for their leaders instead of God are influenced by the spirit of idolatry. The leader is literally worshipped as a god-like figure, and the whole congregation is expected to reverence the leader in this way. This can also happen when a leader is exceptionally gifted, and people are so in awe of the gifts in them as opposed to the giver of the gift who is God: *Therefore, my beloved, run [keep far, far away] from [any sort of] idolatry [and that includes loving anything more than God, or participating in anything that leads to sin and enslaves the soul] (*1 Corinthians 10:14*; AMP).*

Churches and groups characterised by an ungodly reverence of their leaders, usually due to their spiritual gifting, speaking abilities, charismatic personalities, etc., are possibly being influenced by such spirits. There is nothing wrong with the attributes mentioned above. However, placing people on a pedestal because of these attributes is very dangerous. God absolutely detests anything that takes His place as a focus of reverence or worship other than Himself. This kind of spirit operating in a ministry gives rise to all manner of problems and abuses as the leader is literally allowed to get away with anything whilst people passively collude with their sinful behaviour and attribute it to "honouring" or "serving" God.

So, to summarise some of the ways Satan attacks the Church:

1. Sin in the church family - the unresolved and repetitive sins of spiritual parents or leaders will open doorways of demonic influence into the church family's life.

2. Spirits of lust and perversion - Sexually motivated acts by those in leadership or failure to deal with it in the congregation can open doors of spiritual defilement in a church. However, they are not limited to penetrative sex but may include fondling, kissing, lewd conversations, voyeurism, pornography, etc.

3. Deceiving spirits - A leader who has departed from the faith whilst still operating in their position is being influenced by deceiving spirits and will inevitably promote doctrines of devils.

4. Spirits of doubt and unbelief in healing - A church that does not teach healing from sickness is more prone to accepting the enemy's lies and premature death in its congregation. (This does not mean to say we should not seek medical advice).

5. Spirit of fear - Leadership influenced by a spirit of fear can leave open doorways for other spirits of compromise, passivity, people pleasing, etc., to form satanic strongholds over a church or group.

6. The spirit of idolatry will operate in any ministry where ungodly reverence for their leader is promoted above a reverence for God, which will have huge consequences.

Chapter 8

Forgiveness

We will consider a vital topic, **forgiveness**. Now, this tends to be a misunderstood topic for some people and is probably one of the biggest stumbling blocks for believers when they have been hurt in the context of church. Any person who has experienced hurt by others will need to forgive them for healing from their pain. This is needed for them to be spiritually released from the negative consequences that unforgiveness can bring.

Reasons people struggle to forgive:

- They do not understand what forgiveness really means.
- The enemy has used their unforgiveness to set up a spiritual stronghold in their life, which has grown into bitterness.
- They believe forgiveness is just a one-time event.
- They feel that, in some way, their unforgiveness is a way of punishing the other person.
- They are not actually aware or simply do not care that unforgiveness is a sin and has consequences.

Why do we need to forgive?

We are commanded by scripture to forgive others:

> *Then Peter came to Him and said, "Lord, how often shall my brother sin against me, and I forgive him? Up to seven times?" Jesus said to him, "I do not say to you, up to seven times, but up to seventy times seven* (**Matthew 18:21-22**; *NKJV).*

This verse does not suggest we keep counting how many times we forgive someone and retaliate when the limit is reached. Instead, it is saying that forgiveness is unlimited. The Jewish people in those days understood that the phrase seventy times seven means unending, unlimited.

Unforgiveness is sin and has spiritual consequences

Forgiveness is a spiritual law that releases us from the pain of our past hurts but refusing to forgive has consequences:

> *For if you forgive others their trespasses [their reckless and wilful sins], your heavenly Father will also forgive you. But if you do not forgive others [nurturing your hurt and anger with the result that it interferes with your relationship with God], then your Father will not forgive your trespasses (***Matthew 6:14-15***; AMP).*

> *For this reason, I am telling you, whatever things you ask for in prayer [in accordance with God's will], believe [with confident trust] that you have received them, and they will be given to you. Whenever you stand praying, if you have anything against anyone, forgive*

> *him [drop the issue, let it go], so that your*
> *Father who is in heaven will also forgive you*
> *your transgressions and wrongdoings [against*
> *Him and others]. [But if you do not forgive,*
> *neither will your Father in heaven forgive your*
> *transgressions."]* (**Mark 11:24-26**; *AMP*).

These few verses explain that if a person holds onto unforgiveness, God is unable to forgive them. Therefore, we are to let go of anything we have against others, no matter how wrongfully they acted against us:

> *Therefore, be merciful, just as your Father*
> *also is merciful. "Judge not, and you shall not*
> *be judged. Condemn not, and you shall not be*
> *condemned. Forgive, and you will be forgiven*
> (**Luke 6:36-37**; *NKJV*).

Forgiving others has a direct correlation with God's forgiveness towards us. Consequently, our relationship with God is greatly affected by our relationship with others and how much we choose to forgive them or not.

Forgiveness removes demonic spiritual rights over us

Satan and his demons are legalists. In other words, they will use any spiritual rights or the breaking of God's spiritual laws that are open to them because of sin to enter a person's life. *"Be angry, and do not sin": do not let the sun go down on your wrath, nor give place to the devil"* (**Ephesians 4:26-27**; *NKJV*).

Anger is a valid feeling when others do us wrong, but a sinful response because of our anger will permit the enemy spiritual access into our lives.

> *When you forgive anyone, I do too. And whatever I have forgiven (to the extent that this affected me too) has been by Christ's authority, and for your good. A further reason for forgiveness is to keep from being outsmarted by Satan, for we know what he is trying to do (***2 Corinthians 2:10-11***; TLB).*

Unforgiveness gives Satan an advantage over us, and he will enforce his spiritual rights and use it to keep us in bondage. The enemy will fully utilise any doorways we open through unforgiveness against us.

Forgiveness allows healing emotionally and sometimes physically

> *When He saw their faith, He said to him, "Man, your sins are forgiven you." And the scribes and the Pharisees began to reason, saying, "Who is this who speaks blasphemies? Who can forgive sins but God alone?" But when Jesus perceived their thoughts, He answered and said to them, "Why are you reasoning in your hearts? Which is easier, to say, 'Your sins are forgiven you,' or to say, 'Rise up and walk'? But that you may know that the Son of Man has power on earth to forgive sins"—He said to the man who was paralyzed, "I say to you, arise, take up your bed, and go to your house" (***Luke 5:20-24***; NKJV).*

Forgiveness has benefits to our spirit and emotions, but it can also bring release from physical ailments.

Let me share a testimony of healing through forgiveness. Several years ago, a lady in our fellowship arrived at service one Sunday morning in excruciating back pain and was clearly struggling to walk properly. Towards the end of the service, I felt led to pray for her, as the Holy Spirit prompted me to ask if she had anyone she needed to forgive. She opened her eyes wide in surprise and immediately answered yes. I led her in a prayer of forgiveness, and before she could even say Amen, she let out a scream and fell to the ground. After a few moments, she opened her eyes, looked up at me, sat up, and said in amazement: *it's gone; it's gone!* I helped her up off the floor, and she broke out in tears of joy and started praising God. She had been instantly healed from her back problem; the pain had totally gone, and she could walk normally once again. To this day, the problem nor the pain has never returned.

Of course, not every physical condition is a result of unforgiveness or the reason why healing is blocked. However, I'm certain that the Lord will reveal where it is, which can then be prayed into.

Now, we will consider a biblical story that explains the spiritual consequences of harbouring unforgiveness:

> *Therefore, the kingdom of heaven is like a certain king who wanted to settle accounts with his servants. And when he had begun to settle accounts, one was brought to him who owed him ten thousand talents. But as he was not able to pay, his master commanded that he be sold, with his wife and children and all that he had, and that payment be made. The servant therefore fell down before him, saying, 'Master, have patience with me, and I will pay you all.' Then the master of that servant was moved with compassion, released him, and*

*forgave him the debt. "But that servant went out and found one of his fellow servants who owed him a hundred denarii; and he laid hands on him and took him by the throat, saying, 'Pay me what you owe!' So, his fellow servant fell down at his feet and begged him, saying, 'Have patience with me, and I will pay you all.' And he would not but went and threw him into prison till he should pay the debt. So when his fellow servants saw what had been done, they were very grieved, and came and told their master all that had been done. Then his master, after he had called him, said to him, 'You wicked servant! I forgave you all that debt because you begged me. Should you not also have had compassion on your fellow servant, just as I had pity on you?' And his master was angry and delivered him to the torturers until he should pay all that was due to him. "So My heavenly Father also will do to you if each of you, from his heart, does not forgive his brother his trespasses." (***Matthew 18:23-35****; NKJV*).*

Notice it starts by saying that the Kingdom of heaven is like a certain king that wants to settle his accounts. We can extrapolate from this that this is exactly how God operates. So, what does this tell us about forgiveness?

- When we ask God for forgiveness, He completely forgives us.
- Unforgiveness towards others puts us in spiritual torment and bondage.
- God will deal with us similarly to how we choose to forgive or refuse to forgive others.

We can see from the scriptures so far that forgiveness is a commandment; in other words, an order. It is not a suggestion or a good idea; it is a commandment! As believers, it is something we are required to obey; otherwise, we are going against scripture and disobeying God. Sometimes, people hurt us not because they planned to, but because they are so hurt and wounded themselves. They are operating and responding to the world and others out of pain and brokenness. We may think we know exactly why a person has done something to us, but only God really knows an individual's heart. Hurt people, hurt people because they are wounded in some way and don't know any better.

> *And when they had come to the place called Calvary, there they crucified Him, and the criminals, one on the right hand and the other on the left. Then Jesus said, "Father, forgive them, for they do not know what they do..."* **(Luke 23:33-34**; *NKJV).*

> *Those who mocked, spat on, jeered at and crucified Jesus did not understand why they were compelled and driven to do evil or the consequences of it. Sometimes, someone sinning against us may result from some demonic doorway in their own life, and they are driven to do evil. Then, of course, some are very calculated in their evil agenda and fully aware of what they plan to do and their desired outcome. They may believe that their thoughts and plans are of their own doing and could not possibly be influenced by anything other than their own selves. Whatever the reason behind a person's actions, God always*

*expects us to forgive them for our own sakes, not theirs. If someone says, "I love God," and hates his brother, he is a liar; for he who does not love his brother whom he has seen, how can he love God whom he has not seen? (***1 John 4:20***; NKJV).*

A real measure of our relationship with God is how we respond to situations in life that have caused us great pain, especially when it is at the hands of fellow believers or our leaders.

What are some indicators of unforgiveness?

a) A desire to make the other person pay for what they did, taking revenge—of course, when it comes to a crime, it needs to be reported.

b) Character assassination of the other person: continually repeating to others what happened long after the event. There is a place for speaking about our pain to other mature believers who can pray with us or during counselling. But a person's motivation for rehearsing the events and who they choose to share it with is quite telling.

c) Feelings of not being able to get on with life, feeling stuck.

d) Whenever the person's name is mentioned, or you see them in person, feelings of rage, anger, resentment, or hatred rise from within.

e) Refusing to accept an apology from the other person.

This list is not exhaustive, and there may be other signs that a person is holding onto unforgiveness, but these are just a few indicators. If a person holds onto unforgiveness,

there is also the danger that it may develop into bitterness if
not dealt with scripturally:

> Pursue peace with all people, and holiness,
> without which no one will see the Lord: looking
> carefully lest anyone fall short of the grace of
> God; lest any root of bitterness springing up
> cause trouble, and by this many become defiled
> (**Hebrews 12:14-15**; NKJV).

Bitterness has the effect of spreading through the
ear gates of other people, especially if they are not mature
believers. This may cause them to also become defiled by
what they hear. It will inevitably cause them to harbour
unforgiveness towards someone who has not done anything
wrong to them personally. A person may attempt to justify
spreading the information, but the real motive is often to get
revenge and cause others to join their ungodly camp of hatred
and bitterness towards the offender. No amount of repeating
the offence to others will deal with the pain of the hurt; only
true forgiveness can begin the process and bring healing.

Misunderstandings about forgiveness

1. Forgiving someone who has wronged us means
   they will get away with what they did.

No, in reality, we are releasing ourselves from any
negative spiritual attachments to them and letting God deal
with them in His own way and time.

> Don't quarrel with anyone. Be at peace with
> everyone, just as much as possible. Dear
> friends, never avenge yourselves. Leave that to
> God, for he has said that he will repay those

who deserve it. Don't take the law into your own hands. Instead, feed your enemy if he is hungry. If he is thirsty give him something to drink and you will be "heaping coals of fire on his head." In other words, he will feel ashamed of himself for what he has done to you (**Romans 12:18-20**; *TLB).*

2. Forgiveness means I should attempt to reconcile with someone who has hurt me.

No, forgiveness does not mean putting yourself back in a vulnerable situation with someone unsafe and abusive. Likewise, forgiveness does not mean you must reconcile with someone to forgive them. Instead, it concerns your personal relationship with God. Furthermore, it may not be safe to attempt any sort of reconciliation as the person may not have changed and will therefore still repeatedly act in ways towards you that are hurtful or abusive.

3. Forgiveness means I should NOT report the other person's crime against me to the police or authorities.

Not true. A person can forgive someone who has committed a crime against them and still testify against them in court. If a crime has been committed against you or anyone else for that matter, forgiveness does not mean you should not report it to the police.

4. Forgiveness is a bit like sweeping it under the carpet as if it were inconsequential.

Not true. What happened to you is not inconsequential to God. He just wants you to hand it over to Him to deal with: *Beloved, do not avenge yourselves, but rather give place to wrath; for it is written, "Vengeance is Mine, I will repay," says the Lord* (**Romans 12:19**; NKJV). God knows how to deal with situations far better than we do.

Often, when someone has hurt us, understandably, we want to see them punished. However, taking things into our own hands can have disastrous consequences, especially if we are operating from a place of deep anger. Therefore, we must trust God to deal with the situation as He sees fit. Our contribution in the process will depend on individual circumstances as to whether we need to be involved again with the offender.

5. The other person needs to apologise for what they did first before I apologise

Not true. This is a misunderstanding of what biblical forgiveness is about. God does not command us to forgive based on the other person's apology or response to us. This would potentially leave us in limbo. What if the other person never apologises or has died? Some people feel this is the only way to get closure, but this is purely a deception and a misunderstanding of the need to forgive, regardless of the other person's actions.

God never expects the other person to apologise to us for us to forgive them, even though an apology would be nice from our human perspective. Ultimately, forgiveness is about our relationship with God. It is between us and God, not us and the other person who has wronged us.

Forgiving God

This may sound like an oxymoron, as God cannot sin. Therefore, He is in no need of our forgiveness. Nevertheless, sometimes, people may blame God for all the bad things that have happened to them, especially in a church context. They may not actually verbalise this, but questions in their heart may be like: "God, why did you allow this to happen to me?" or "Where was God if He really cared about me?" Although God does not need to repent, we must ask for His forgiveness for wrongfully blaming Him for what we have suffered: *"God is not a man, that He should lie, Nor a son of man, that He should repent. Has He said, and will He not do? Or has He spoken, and will He not make it good? (***Numbers 23:19***; NKJV).*

The reality of forgiveness

The reality about forgiveness is that a person will have to live with the consequences of what was done and may be unable to change anything, e.g., the murder of a loved one. Forgiveness will not bring them back to life. Another instance is being ejected from a ministry because of slander and lies. Forgiving those who have hurt you will not necessarily repair the damaged relationships, which may be lost forever.

As painful as it may be, you will have to trust God and get on with your life as best as possible with a forgiving heart. It may seem unfair, but the only choice is to live in the bondage of bitterness or the freedom of forgiveness. Unless a person forgives from their heart, they will be unable to benefit from the deliverance or healing that forgiveness enables a person to enjoy.

Rest assured, if you have had the misfortune of being misused, abused, ill-treated, belittled, shunned, rejected, or hurt in any way in the context of church, God is not happy about it. However, there is life after church hurt or spiritual abuse, and God wants to restore the life of anyone who has suffered at the hands of others, whether they are leaders or fellow believers. Forgiveness is a potent and effective way God has given to us, enabling healing when church or other situations have hurt us deeply. If a person really wants to live a life free from past hurts, they will need to obey God's commandment to forgive. The level to which they are willing to do this greatly impacts their relationship with God. It will bring tremendous freedom and a great sense of release into their life.

Conclusions about forgiveness:

1. Forgiveness is a commandment from God which must be obeyed.

2. Unforgiveness has spiritual consequences; it ties us to the other person and can become bitterness.

3. Forgiveness removes any rights that Satan has over us.

4. Forgiveness is about our relationship with God and is not reliant on the other person's apology or our need for so-called closure.

5. A person cannot effectively heal spiritually without forgiving first. It may also bring physical healing in certain circumstances.

6. A person may need God's forgiveness for wrongfully blaming Him.

7. Ultimately, the choice is ours to find freedom in forgiveness or be bound in unforgiveness and bitterness.

Chapter 9

The Importance of the Body of Christ

Due to being hurt in its various forms within a church context, it is completely understandable why a person would want absolutely nothing to do with church. This is a highly well-executed plan of the enemy to use their negative experiences and convince them with reasonable arguments that being part of a church group is not a good idea. What they may not have tuned into whilst processing their hurt and pain is that Jesus Christ instituted the Church despite the flaws of some of its members. Although parts of the Body of Christ may appear not to be functioning very well, being a part of the body in a healthy context is what God desires for all His people.

Just like a human body, an individual limb was never designed to function detached from the main body. So likewise, Jesus Christ desired everyone to be attached to the Body of Christ and function the way He intended. The Church was not man's idea. It was never designed to be numerous and separate religious institutions, but a living, thriving body of people with Christ being the head: *And God has put all things under his feet and made him the supreme Head of the Church (**Ephesians 1:22**; TLB).*

*Instead, we will lovingly follow the truth at all times—speaking truly, dealing truly, living truly—and so become more and more in every way like Christ who is the Head of his body, the Church. Under his direction, the whole body is fitted together perfectly, and each part in its own special way helps the other parts, so that the whole body is healthy and growing and full of love' (***Ephesians 4:15-16***; TLB).*

Just like our bodies were designed to function as a whole unit despite having many individual parts, so was the Church intended to perform with many members, but as one united body of believers. Can you imagine the various parts of the body deciding to operate separately? They would have a tough time functioning without the rest of the body and would never be able to fulfil their potential if the various members were not properly attached.

Let's look at how the Bible describes the importance of the human body and the parallels between it and the Church body:

For just as the body is one and yet has many parts, and all the parts, though many, form [only] one body, so it is with Christ. For by one [Holy] Spirit we were all baptized into one body, [spiritually transformed—united together] whether Jews or Greeks (Gentiles), slaves or free, and we were all made to drink of one [Holy] Spirit [since the same Holy Spirit fills each life]. If the foot says, "Because I am not a hand, I am not a part of the body," is it not on the contrary still a part of the body? If the ear says, "Because I am not an eye, I am not a part of the body," is it not on the contrary still a part of the body? If the whole body were an eye, where would the hearing be? If the whole [body] were an ear, where would the sense of smell be? But now [as things really are], God has placed and arranged the parts in the body, each one of them, just as He willed and saw fit [with the best balance of function]. If they all were a single organ, where would [the rest of] the body be? But now [as things really are] there are many parts [different limbs and organs], but a single body. The eye cannot say to the hand, "I have no need of you," nor again the head to the feet, "I have no need of you." But quite the contrary, the parts of the body that seem to be weaker are [absolutely] necessary; and as for those parts of the body which we consider less honorable, these we treat with greater honor; and our less presentable parts are treated with greater modesty, while our more presentable parts do not require it. But God has combined the [whole] body, giving greater honor to that part which lacks it, so that there would be no division or discord in the body [that is, lack of adaptation of the parts to each other], but that the parts may have the same concern for one another. And if one member suffers, all the parts share the suffering; if one member is honored, all rejoice with it (**1 Corinthians 12:12-26**; *AMP*).

What do these verses tell us?

1. Any part of the body feeling insignificant because it is not another part does not mean it is not part of the body.

2. No part of the body can say to any other part that they are not needed.

3. Even those parts of the body that may seem to be weak are vitally important.

4. Parts of the body that seem less respectable should be given greater respect.

5. Some parts need greater modesty and care, whilst others do not.

6. God gives greater honour to the part which lacks, enabling the parts to work together happily.

7. Whatever affects one part of the body impacts the entire body, whether negative or positive.

God designed the human body to function in a particular way, and absolutely every part has an important role to play in harmony with the rest of the body. Our human body is made up of many parts. Some are external, like arms, hands, legs, ears, nose, and eyes, and can easily be seen. Our private parts are normally covered but are equally important. Our internal organs like the heart, liver, and lungs are all hidden inside but have indispensably significant roles in the successful functioning of the entire body. If any of these internal organs were to stop working, it would seriously affect the rest of the body.

Even though these organs are working behind the scenes, as it were, this does not minimise their importance to the whole body. Equally so, every person in the Body of Christ is vitally important. Nobody is insignificant. So, therefore, any person trying to operate on their own away from the Body of Christ will not be functioning in line with God's divine purpose for the Church body. Just like an eye could not leave the body and function by itself, individual members of the Body of Christ must function in line with the way God intended. There is a concerted demonic agenda to separate people from being attached to the Body of Christ, which causes the body to be deformed and disabled.

Some believers sincerely believe they can serve God by themselves, and yes, we are all called to make a personal decision to accept Jesus Christ as individuals. Still, it is a deception to believe that we can do what God has called us to do alone, in isolation from the rest of the body. Often, people who have been hurt in the context of church totally reject any committed association with the Church body or simply church-hop whenever it suits them. Their view of the Church has become skewed as a version with nothing to do with the One who instituted it. Jesus Christ and their personal view become their model for how they now choose to do "church". Sadly, they are more than likely operating from a wounded heart, which if not healed effectively, will distort their thinking, causing them to make wrong decisions about their spiritual future. They may not personally see it in this light, but if they are not aligning themselves with the body of believers that Christ intended, they are disadvantaged in their faith or simply do not understand what the biblical church is about. Whatever their reasons, they are merely attempting to practice a form of non-community Christianity that Jesus never intended His people to embrace.

Charles Colson, in his book, *The Body*, echoes similar sentiments:

> *...it is scandalous that so many believers today have such a low view of church. They see their*

Christian lives as a solitary exercise—Jesus and me—or they treat the church as a building or a social centre. They flit from congregation to congregation—or they don't associate with any church at all. That the church is held in such low esteem reflects not only the depts of our biblical ignorance, but the alarming extent to which we have succumbed to the obsessive individualism of modern culture (Colson, 1992:276).

There may be instances where a person is physically unable to be part of a local fellowship for legitimate reasons. However, to decide not to attend any church fellowship whatsoever and believe that one can honestly serve God is a strong delusion. Scripture reveals that we serve Christ as part of the Body of Christ, not in isolation. Consequently, a person towing such a path simply disobeys scripture if they choose to do things their own way and not biblically.

...any Christian who has a choice in the matter, failure to cleave to a particular church is failure to obey Christ. For it is only through a confessing, local body of believers that we carry out the work of the church in the world (Colson, 1992:277).

The importance of the church community

When it comes to spiritual gifts, they are distributed by God to individuals so they can complement each other as a community of believers. Let's consider what the apostle Paul says about using spiritual gifts within the context of the Body of Christ:

*For I say, through the grace given to me, to everyone who is among you, not to think of himself more highly than he ought to think, but to think soberly, as God has dealt to each one a measure of faith. For as we have many members in one body, but all the members do not have the same function, so we, being many, are one body in Christ, and individually members of one another. Having then gifts differing according to the grace that is given to us, let us use them: if prophecy, let us prophesy in proportion to our faith; or ministry, let us use it in our ministering; he who teaches, in teaching; he who exhorts, in exhortation; he who gives, with liberality; he who leads, with diligence; he who shows mercy, with cheerfulness (***Romans 12:3-8**; *NKJV).*

Paul starts by talking about individual members being part of one body, then immediately, in verse six, moves on to talk about spiritual gifts. In other words, whichever gift God has given us, we should use it to complement each other in the context of the body for the benefit of all. He parallels the Body of Christ with the human body and puts across his point that there are many members but one body. The place for us to exercise and practice our gifts is within the community of the Body of Christ, not as lone rangers and in isolation. God gives gifts to individuals for us to function together as one body. The gifts were not given so that individual limbs, as it were, could benefit for themselves.

They are supposed to benefit the entire body by working together in humility. No matter where God has placed us in the body or what gifting we have, we should never see ourselves as better or more significant than other members. Instead, we must recognise that we are there to complement one another in the spirit of love and unity in a community of fellow believers. *In this community our gifts are developed and exercised...If we don't grasp the intrinsically corporate nature of Christianity embodied in the church, we are missing the very heart of Jesus' plan* (Colson, 1992:277).

What does all of this tell us?

1. Many different persons make up the entire body
2. Every person is relevant, and it takes all of us to make it complete
3. Every person has a different part to play in the body
4. We belong to each other and need each other
5. Each person has God-given gifts to complement other gifted individuals

Leadership regarding the body

The Apostle Paul talks about the purpose of church leadership in conjunction with the entire Body of Christ: *And He Himself gave some to be apostles, some prophets, some evangelists, and some pastors and teachers, for the equipping of the saints for the work of ministry, for the edifying of the body of Christ,* (**Ephesians 4:11-12**; NKJV). The word "edify" simply means to enlighten, inform, educate, instruct, improve, or teach. Therefore, the role of leadership is to edify the entire Body of Christ. It is a gift from God to benefit the whole Body of Christ, not just certain parts. The Bible constantly repeats this parallel between the human body and the Church body so we can understand God's purpose for us functioning within a church community of believers. So, if we think about the human body and keeping individual limbs healthy, we do not need to detach an injured part to work on it. It is always attached to the body, whether it needs healing, nutrients, exercise, or rest.

It is equally so with the Church body; we do not thrive as individual parts. We thrive together as a united body of believers. The greatest ploy against the Body of Christ is separating individual persons, convincing them they do not need the rest of the body, especially when they have been hurt. His method for doing this is to use other persons in the Body of Christ to cause offence and hurt people. Sadly, all too often, it is from a leader or the leadership: *"Beware of false prophets, who come to you in sheep's clothing, but inwardly they are ravenous wolves"* (**Matthew 7:15**; NKJV). An individual separated from the Body of Christ is weaker, less enthusiastic about the Church, and far more vulnerable to the enemy, making it more difficult to reattach to the body again. *Be sober [well balanced and self-disciplined], be alert and cautious at all times. That enemy of yours, the devil, prowls around like a roaring lion [fiercely hungry], seeking someone to devour* (**1 Peter 5:8**; AMP).

Satan will work through individuals to attack the flock and cause them to separate from the rest of the body, thereby making them more vulnerable. For instance, an individual will be presented with various reasons they should stay away, but this is purely a demonic deception, as the Church was designed for individuals to function together in a community as one body.

> *Therefore if there is any encouragement and comfort in Christ [as there certainly is in abundance], if there is any consolation of love, if there is any fellowship [that we share] in the Spirit, if [there is] any [great depth of] affection*

*and compassion, make my joy complete by
being of the same mind, having the same love
[toward one another], knit together in spirit,
intent on one purpose [and living a life that
reflects your faith and spreads the gospel—the
good news regarding salvation through faith
in Christ]* **(Philippians 2:1-2***; AMP).*

The body of believers, the Church, is vitally important.
Therefore, the enemy will use every ploy possible to keep
people away from the Body of Christ because of hurts and
negative things they have experienced. However, once a
person truly understands the purpose and God's desired
function for His body of believers, they will be able to see
more clearly why the enemy orchestrates things to keep
them separated.

Conclusions:

1. The Church, which is the Body of Christ, was
   instituted by God Himself, with Jesus Christ as
   the head.

2. Leadership is given to the Church as gifts in the
   form of apostles, prophets, evangelists, pastors,
   and teachers to equip all the saints and edify the
   entire body.

3. God places all individuals within the Body of Christ
   as He sees fit.

4. Just like a human body, each part is significant and
   needs to work together with the rest of the body as
   one unit.

5. Spiritual gifts are given to individuals as God sees
   fit, which complements other believers for the
   benefit of the Body of Christ.

6. It is a satanic deception for people to believe that they can truly operate in the will of God whilst separated from the Body of Christ.

7. We all need each other to carry out the functions of the body, and everyone should feel important, appreciated, and loved.

Chapter 10

My Personal Story

Early Childhood

I was introduced to the Bible as a child in Sunday school at around the age of five years and remember hearing stories of Noah's ark and Joseph's coat of many colours. Although I found them interesting, I did not properly understand their significance, they were only stories to me. It would be about another twenty-two years before I was introduced to Jesus Christ. My childhood memories were filled with things that no child should ever experience. I had been sexually abused by an older boy between the ages of four and six. I also suffered additional emotional and physical abuse because of the domestic violence prevalent in our home. Not surprisingly, I developed deep-seated insecurities about myself and struggled to understand why my father hated me so much and would constantly accuse my mother and me of plotting against him. He treated me differently from my younger brother, who was his favourite. I had no idea that he was suffering from mental health issues, which would only be formerly diagnosed many years later.

I remember one occasion at around age five or six when my father took me into the kitchen to punish me, locking the door behind us. I was made to strip naked, fold my clothes neatly, and place them on a chair before he beat me with a leather strap. Crying was not an option, as I was told that any tears would make things worse for me. From then onwards, I developed an ability to keep my emotions inside and had no choice but to put up with the abuse. The trauma of the abuse was indelibly imprinted in my psyche and would play itself out well into my adult years. This meant that keeping things to myself became an automatic default response to difficult situations. I felt helpless as I witnessed my mother being beaten by my father on numerous occasions. I thought I should do something about it, but at such a young age, the expectations of my ability to intervene were immaturely unrealistic. Nevertheless, I still felt heavily responsible, even at six years old.

This all stopped for a window of three years when my mother decided to take my brother and me to live with my maternal grandparents outside of London, following an incident where my father purposely threw a saucepan of boiling hot water at her, scolding her arm. Unknown to me, my father was arrested and went to prison for several months for the assault. The next three years were delightful for me as a child, and I was free from the toxic atmosphere I had been used to until then. Despite this, the psychological and emotional damage had already been done and was becoming obvious. A family member commented to my mother that we needed to be kept away from our father, as we were displaying signs of being affected by his abusive behaviour. One of my schoolteachers also discerned that something was wrong and told my mother that I needed to be encouraged to play more with the boys instead of constantly fighting them.

I guess in my own way, I was re-enacting what I had already learned, and my aggression towards my male peers would cause them to avoid me at all costs. I had no idea that their rejection of me resulted from my behaviour, and

I resigned myself to playing with the girls instead. I enjoyed living with my grandparents and had younger cousins and teenage uncles who lived there, too. We were well looked after, felt loved and secure, and my grandmother became like a second mother to me. Those would be the only truly happy years of my childhood.

After three years, things changed again. My father was now out of prison and was attempting to reconcile with my mother. Occasionally, my brother and I would stay with my father at his new home in London. I detested those visits, as I had no connection with my father. He would take us on visits to one of his girlfriends and thought nothing of kissing them on the lips in front of us and complaining to them about our mother. He had no sense of what was appropriate and acted and spoke in ways that were not conducive to the emotional well-being of his two young children. At age nine, my mother decided to give my father another chance, so we left the security of my grandparents' home and moved in with my father to our new home in Southeast London. Inevitably, things would get much worse.

Growing Up

I was brilliant as a child despite my abusive situation at home, and the headmistress at my junior school noticed this and suggested to my parents that they should send me to a grammar school near central London. It was a highly sought-after naval school, and it was difficult to get admitted. However, I passed the entry exams and was offered a place. We wore a black naval type of uniform with brass buttons on the jacket, which made it very distinguishable from more standard school uniforms, and we also wore a cap. We had to stand on parade every morning for fifteen minutes in the playground, where other senior boys inspected our uniforms, caps, and shoes, and would give out appropriate punishments if things were not in order under the watchful supervision of the headmaster.

I learned to play the clarinet, which I was very good at, and picked things up very quickly. I was also very good at maths and came top in my class in the first year to my astonishment. However, I wanted to continue learning the clarinet, and my one-to-one clarinet lessons clashed with one of my maths lessons. I thoroughly enjoyed learning music, and the school allowed me to take home a clarinet to practice. My parents had to sign for this, and one day, my father discovered I was skipping one maths lesson per week to learn the clarinet. He immediately stopped it, declaring that maths was far more important, and my days of playing the clarinet ended abruptly. I was devastated. Another music teacher noticed I had a good singing voice and put me forward to audition for a cathedral choir not too far from our school. It was a rather prestigious Anglican church near central London, and a small handful of us were accepted as choristers, along with a few other boys from other grammar schools in London.

I really enjoyed singing, and it also offered me an opportunity to be out of the home for choir practice one evening per week. We would also be required to sing for both the morning and evening services on Sundays, which enabled me to be out of the home the whole day. In between services, we had time for recreation, playing table tennis or pool, and were always fed a tasty Sunday roast which I looked forward to. I made friends easily and felt valued as they would often put new boys next to me to learn their notes whilst listening to me. Unfortunately, I began noticing that the same boys I was mentoring were also being promoted above me. It soon became apparent that I was denied promotion due to my skin colour. This was my earliest recollection of racism and experiencing such treatment in a church made it more memorable as it was the last place in the world, I would have expected it.

Annually, the whole choir was taken on a weeklong camping trip during the summer holidays to Devon, England. I attended one and was looking forward to being away from all the negativity at home. However, whilst away on this trip, I noticed one of the priests who accompanied us hanging around some of the boys' tents during the evenings at bedtimes. I remember hearing other boys giggling and laughing as he fooled around with them in their tents. What later transpired was that he was playing sexualised games with them that included seeing how far he could get his hands down inside their pyjama legs before they could stop him. Though I did not understand the significance of what I heard then, I now realise that this priest was a child sexual abuser. On my return home, I told my mother I did not want to go on anymore camping trips with the church, although I never explained why. Soon afterwards, I decided to make a complaint again to my choirmaster about the unfair treatment of promoting newer boys above me. One of my fellow white choristers also noticed the way I was being ill treated and accompanied me to complain. I was told, *"If you do not like it, then you know what you can do"*. We were both ejected from the choir that day. I had no personal relationship with Jesus Christ at the time and was not a believer, and the harrowing experiences would tarnish my views about church for a long time.

On one occasion, my father attacked my mother with a piece of wood which had a nail sticking out of it. She had grabbed hold of it to defend herself, and the nail went into her hand. She was bleeding profusely, and I accompanied her to the hospital for medical treatment and stitches. On the way there, she shouted at me, *"Why didn't you stop him?"* I was stunned into silence. I felt like a failure for not protecting my mother; somehow, I became like a "surrogate husband" from then onwards. I was eleven years old, the one she confided in, and whose job it was to try and console her. I knew my mum really loved me, but in her own brokenness due to unresolved childhood trauma, she did not feel confident about leaving my father again and taking us with her for fear of being unable to cope. I am sure she would have managed if she had, but unfortunately, we would never know.

Teenage years

Things at home continued to deteriorate. My father's abusive treatment of my mother was a regular occurrence, and he also directed much of his abuse towards me. Finally, at the age of thirteen, he suggested I should commit suicide because nobody wanted me, and that I would be doing everyone a great favour. I felt so broken and utterly rejected by his angry words that I decided I would kill myself. I got as far as standing with one foot outside my bedroom window, but I was crying so bitterly that I could not clearly see where I would land four storeys below. It may sound silly now, but at the time, it was literally the one thought that stopped me from jumping. I eventually climbed back into the bedroom and sat on my bed, sobbing uncontrollably and depression became a dark cloud that would hang over me for years to come.

I felt like I was living in hell; the constant verbal abuse and domestic violence created a very toxic, hostile environment, and the only release from this being when my father was at work or I was out of the home in school, or outside playing. I began to hate my father and his constant put-downs. On one occasion, we attended a party at one of his friends' homes. Whilst my mother was out of the room, he started his barrage of verbal abuse against me in front of other adults, saying to them in earshot of me, *"Look at him, he is going to grow up to be a (expletive) little queer, a little sissy"*. This sort of verbal abuse was nothing new to me, and he would often tell me, *"You are just like your (expletive) mother"*. All the unkind words he spoke to me became like daggers in my soul, and all I knew was that it hurt deeply, but I had no way of stopping him or escaping the situation. I had no idea what a "queer" was, but years later, I began hearing the word used against others in school in a derogatory manner. So, I began questioning myself as to who I was. The Bible is so true when it says that "life and death are in the power of the tongue". My father's words gradually killed any sense of worth that I had in me, to the extent that I could not even look in the mirror because I thought I was so very ugly. Then, my self-esteem was exceptionally low. I was often punished for the slightest thing I did wrong, and my father would sometimes make me take a shower, warning me not to lock the door. A few minutes later, he would burst into the bathroom, pull back the curtain, and beat me with a leather belt. I was utterly defenceless against his twisted and brutal forms of punishment and felt totally humiliated. On hindsight, there was something perverse about his methods of punishment, and I often wonder what kinds of abuse he had experienced in his own childhood growing up in the Caribbean.

I was filled with hatred and began fantasising about killing my father in order to put a stop to the living hell I was in. My plan was to wait until he was asleep and then clobber him over the head with a kitchen rolling pin. Thank goodness I never carried out my plans, but this was only due to the fear of him waking up and catching me hovering over him, but

Colin A Mason

the hatred would stay with me for years. It was around this time that my father was officially medically diagnosed with paranoid schizophrenia and placed on medication. However, he often refused to take it, as he was convinced that "they" were trying to control him. I was getting older and bigger and was beginning to take a stance against my father. I remember breaking down the bathroom door he had locked whilst beating my mother on the other side. I continued to be my mother's protector and would increasingly stand up to my father. He still attempted to beat me, though, and on one occasion, I just stood there whilst he took the belt to me and then looked him in the eyes and asked if he had finished yet. On reflection, I believe my father's absolute hatred for me as his oldest son was because I looked so much like him, unlike my younger brother, like a kind of self-hatred. Unsurprisingly, my schoolwork suffered over time because of the atmosphere at home, and my grades dropped, resulting in a beating when my school report arrived at home. The academic potential I had shown initially, evaporated, and there was absolutely no one to help me.

I attempted one time to tell my class teacher what was happening at home and mentioned that my dad had hit my mother. His response was rather cool, and he said something like, *"Try not to let it bother you"*. After that, I never again attempted to speak about the situation to anyone again. Once, the police came to our front door as someone had reported sounds of a woman screaming. It was my mother pleading for mercy, but my father told the police that "*this was a domestic situation, which was none of their (expletive) business*", and slammed the door shut in their face. Of course, things were different back then, and the police were powerless to do anything unless my mother made a complaint herself.

When I was fifteen, my father emigrated to America supposedly to make a better life for "us". He claimed he would send for us once he was settled, and we would all be starting a new life together. I decided to put my plans for any future in the UK on hold in anticipation of us leaving within a year or two. I remember telling my careers officer at school that I did not need any help because I would leave for America soon. However, it never happened. My father never sent for us, and to be honest, deep down inside, I was relieved. The day he left the UK was one of the happiest days in my life. I discovered many years later that my father never had any intentions of sending for us, and when his older brother asked him when he would be sending for his wife and children, his response was, *"As far as I am concerned, they can all rot in England"*. He had effectively lied and abandoned us, but the scars of years of abuse would not leave so easily. It was another fifteen years before I saw my father again. My mother persuaded me to come on a trip to America to meet both sides of our family and encouraged me to see my father. Despite what he had done, she had always encouraged me to try and keep a relationship going with him, so I agreed to go with her. I need not have bothered, although I met many other lovely family members, my few interactions with my father were enormously disappointing.

Free to be me

When my father abandoned us, all restrictions were gone too, and I was free to be myself although I did not really know who I was. I felt safe and free for the first time since leaving the safety of my grandparents' home six years earlier. I started smoking cigarettes, drinking alcohol, smoking weed, and occasionally trying harder drugs like cocaine and heroin. I also enjoyed clubbing with my brother and other friends our age. I thought I was having a great time but had no idea what the enemy was planning for me. I secured my first job at age sixteen at a well-known fast-food chain, earning one pound and fifteen pence per hour. I dated a few girls, but none of my relationships lasted longer than a few weeks. I wasn't that bothered, as I was still trying to discover who I was, and I did not know how very broken I was on the inside. I did various jobs in-between but decided I would prefer an office job and trained to be an office assistant securing a job at a large local hospital as a salaries and wages clerk. It was here that my life would take another turn as a young adult when I met a lady five years older than me, and things seemed to click with her far more than any of my previous girlfriends. We went on a few dates before we ended up in bed together, and months later, I moved in with her. We eventually bought a home together, but I ignored the warning signs that should have alerted me to danger.

We were together for about six years, and my life once again became a living hell. We both entered the relationship with numerous unresolved issues, and she became verbally and physically abusive toward me on many occasions. Due to what I had experienced as a child, I vowed never to hit a woman and tolerated her physical and verbal aggression towards me. I remember going to work one day, and someone else noticed blood seeping through the forearms of my shirt. It was where she had dug her nails into my forearms during an argument that morning, and although I had stopped the bleeding initially, it began seeping through the bandages under my shirt. On another occasion, we had an argument, and she stood over me, holding a cup of hot coffee and threatening to scold my private parts as I lay down. This was not the first time I saw her in such raging anger.

Before we moved in together, I had witnessed her holding a hot iron up to her brother's face in a rage and threatening to burn him. I overlooked numerous other red flags simply because I was in a "steady" relationship and I really wanted to make things work. I felt I had invested a lot in the relationship, plus the fact that we now had a mortgage together. I tried my best, but gradually I became weary and began losing hope. Eventually, things came to a head one day when I snapped and found myself retaliating against her physical aggression and racial slurs and had a flashback of my father beating my mother which stopped me dead in my track. I felt I had turned into what I hated about my father and broke down crying. That was the final straw, and I decided to end the relationship and stay single, although I refused to move out. It was a very hostile atmosphere to remain in, and I became very low as I found myself living once again in a highly toxic environment.

Minister of Unrighteousness

Unknown to me, the enemy had set me up and had further plans to destroy me. In my pursuit of a happy single life and keeping fit, I attracted the attention of an older guy at a local leisure centre that I visited frequently. He was very friendly towards me and invited me to go over the road for a coffee. I remember thinking to myself, "just say no", but before I could stop myself, I heard the word "yes" coming out of my own mouth. Even though he was a complete stranger, I began to open up to him about my failed relationship with my girlfriend and my struggles with unwanted same-sex attractions. It was the first time in my life I had ever spoken about my feelings to anybody else. I felt like I was being freed, and before long, one thing led to another, and we ended up in bed together. I discovered shortly afterwards that he was a minister of an established local church, married with three children and was twenty years my senior. I justified it by believing that "God" was using this man to help me discover myself, but it was clearly Satan deceiving me into believing a lie. Not once did he ever speak to me about God, although I would sometimes help him with church services, preparing for weddings and christenings. I was at college at the time studying for an accountancy qualification, and he supported me financially in purchasing all the required textbooks. I did very well in my exams, coming top of my year with a distinction. My life had changed dramatically, and I was now considering embracing what I believed was a side of myself that I had buried for years. It felt liberating, and I was happy. After all, I had tried a serious long-term relationship with a woman, which had failed miserably and now I was being true to myself or so I thought. Satan had cleverly made a strategic move in my life, but God was about to make His.

Meeting Jesus

Around this time, a family member who had become a born-again Christian started witnessing to me and was constantly inviting me to visit a Christian house group. I was not the slightest bit interested; after all, I had a friend who was a minister, and he was not trying to cram God down my throat. Interestingly, this "minister" friend of my mine tried his best to put me off visiting their group and warned me that they might try and clone me. Although I had ended my relationship with him, we had remained good friends and would hang out with each other periodically, as I found him very easy to talk to. Due to my previous experience of church as a youngster, I wanted nothing to do with anything that even remotely resembled church or Christianity. I felt they were all fakes, and their priests were paedophiles. After all, that was my experience, and nobody could tell me otherwise. I certainly had no desire to enter a church building, but I eventually agreed to visit a house group at a friend's home. To be honest, the main reason for attending was to prove that they were a cult and not be trusted, but I could not deny the presence of God that I encountered whilst attending the Friday night house group meetings. It was a bizarre but exciting phenomenon for me, as I was experiencing something totally different. It was something I had not felt either in Sunday school at age five, or as a chorister around the age of eleven, despite both being in the context of a church.

The fact that I felt the tangible presence of God in such a way in somebody's living room outside of a church building was completely new for me. It stirred up something in me that made me want to know this God more. After a few months of attending the house group meetings, I was challenged to give my life to God. Part of my hesitation was that I had heard of people with same-sex attractions being treated abysmally by Christians. I had no idea what they would think of me if they knew me properly and was keenly aware that at that time in our culture, you dare not speak about such things. I eventually decided to attend the group's church to get baptised as I had run out of excuses as to why I should not. Also, God had even answered some of my prayers for further confirmation through a series of seemingly coincidental non-related events. The day before, I attended a wedding with a friend and smoked my last cigarette and cannabis joint. Sunday morning arrived, and I do not even remember the sermon's content. All I knew was I wanted more of God, so I answered the call to the altar for prayer, and within minutes, I was filled by the power of the Holy Spirit and baptised by full immersion in water later the same day.

I soon got into church life, attended every service I could and was always eager to be fully involved with my new church family. I did not realise it then, but the church's culture gradually seduced me. In some ways, looking back now, thirty years later, I became somewhat of a clone of the religious system that I had become a part of, just like my "minister" friend had warned me about. Don't get me wrong; it was not all bad. I had great experiences; the teaching was good (although some may disagree, considering my story), and the worship and presence of God were phenomenal. I enjoyed the fellowship and was given some accurate prophetic words, some of which are still coming to pass almost thirty years later. The sad thing was that my entire world was centred around the church group due to my immaturity. This affected some of my relationships with family and friends, unless they attended the same church. However, my pastor was a great speaker and had a real heart for evangelism, and I soon became involved in door-knocking and setting up Bible studies to share the gospel. I enjoyed teaching Bible studies and discovered I had a knack for getting people to agree to one, probably due to my previous experience as a door-to-door double glazing salesman in my late teens.

It was a thriving though relatively young church, and those in leadership positions were very young themselves. Many of them did not have the maturity their role required; therefore, some caused a great deal of hurt to others. There were several levels in the hierarchy, and those high up were treated as if they were better or more important than others, or at least, that is how it seemed on reflection. Even the seating arrangements promoted this idea, and certain leaders would get away with behaviours and attitudes that the ordinary church member would not be able to.

Nevertheless, it was regarded as one of London's fastest-growing black Pentecostal churches.

I began having flashbacks of my sexual abuse as a child and felt tormented, especially at night. Soon, a breakdown crept in, and I sobbed uncontrollably, unable to verbalise what was happening, as I simply did not know. Until then, I had no recollection of ever being sexually abused and thought I was going crazy. Finally, I decided to see my pastor and reluctantly shared my struggles and was somewhat comforted that he would support me. He did his best, and I will always be sincerely grateful to him, but looking back, what I desperately needed was deliverance and inner healing. I experienced a certain level of healing at this church because I genuinely felt loved and accepted, but I needed much more. I was coming to terms with the trauma of emerging memories of sexual abuse and the resultant struggles with unwanted bi-sexual feelings and did my best to verbalise this with my pastor. However, I was told in no uncertain terms, *"No, brother; you are definitely fully homosexual"*. It was one of the most devastating pronouncements I have ever had spoken over me. All my other issues—, sexual abuse trauma, pornography, previous relationships with women, drug taking, having an abusive father with mental health issues, and my involvement with the occult—were never explored or prayed into. Let alone the fact that I was still living with my girlfriend outside of wedlock, (this church prided itself on high moral standards and living holy, so this was a big no no) although I was eventually encouraged to move out. What became the focus was my supposed fully fledged "homosexuality". Effectively, this was a lie, but the narrative suited the ministry profile of saving a former "homosexual", and I would eventually become the "ex-homosexual" poster boy.

I was permitted to travel abroad to attend conferences for Christians battling unwanted same-sex attractions and heard a lot of great testimonies and teachings. However, I never once received any in-depth ministry into any of the spiritual baggage affecting me. As I believed his erroneous label of "you are definitely fully homosexual", it caused me to start questioning whether I had been living a lie. Did I really like women? Was I covering up and pretending? It is amazing how the devil can use people to speak lies into your life and how much more dangerous this is when it comes from a spiritual leader I respected and looked up to for guidance. How tragic that in my most vulnerable time, the devil was trying to reinforce those lies by another father-type figure, reinforcing the false labels my father had put on me. To add insult to injury, whilst attending counselling with a Christian organisation that specialises in supporting those that struggle with unwanted same-sex attractions, my male counsellor came onto me. It was not obvious initially, and being my first time in counselling, I had no clue what to expect. I became increasingly uncomfortable with his desire to hug me after each session but assumed this was part of the therapy.

The hugs were becoming increasingly longer and making me uncomfortable, but one day, he suddenly pushed me away after another counsellor came into the room by accident. It was at that point that it dawned on me that his hugs were inappropriate. Thank goodness that nothing other than this happened, and soon after this, the organisation was bombarded with accusations about this same counsellor by several other men. Sadly, in their situations, the counsellor had taken things too far, and someone leaked the story to the media. TV reporters eventually arrived at the building, and the news broke on a programme about fake "ex-gay ministries" on channel four. The branch was soon shut down, and my trust in counselling took a severe blow. However, years later, I would train to be a counsellor myself.

Eventually, I was encouraged to share my testimony with the church as my ex-girlfriend, threatened to tell everybody after I confessed my same-sex attractions to her. Although I agreed to share my story with the church, it permanently labelled me as an "ex-homosexual", a status I seriously came to regret. Years later, I was paraded on stage at our annual church conference in a shocking attempt to boast about the ministry and its ability to save the gutter most of sinners. I felt rather used as if my story ranked higher in importance than me personally and the way it was done was more for sensationalism. I soon experienced the consequences of such inappropriate public exposure, when one of the conference's guest speakers from America totally ignored me in the corridor afterwards when I went to shake his hand. The next day, the same guest speaker ignorantly said during his message to the conference that my testimony would open the ministry to the spirit of homosexuality coming in. It was a totally ignorant and inappropriate statement for a guest speaker to make at our conference, but it was never challenged nor corrected. My future fiancée would one day share with me that she cringed when she heard me "testifying" at the conference and felt then what I later painfully realised: I was being used terribly in a publicly humiliating manner.

During my time at that church, I had developed a rather ungodly attitude towards other ministries that were not like ours and worshipped differently. I would often make comparisons and pridefully judge other ministries even though I was attending to get help and support. I had indeed taken on board the ungodly culture of my church group without realising it. In my mind, I had come to believe that only our group knew how to properly worship and serve God, that only our organisation had biblically sound doctrine. I had developed what I would now consider a toxic religious mindset. On attending one of these meetings, and with an attitude that was very dismissive of other types of worship, God warned me about my attitude during one of their "comparatively" sedate worship services. He told me off for my ungodly attitude towards my brothers and sisters in Christ, saying, *"Don't you dare ever think that you have a monopoly on worshipping Me"*. His words startled me and initiated a very slow process of considering things from His perspective. However, it would still take many more years to be delivered from the extremely judgmental religious mindset that had become a part of me.

Throughout all of this, I enjoyed Church; the services were excellent, and God's Spirit tangibly moved amongst us. Soon, I began to realise that I was starting to flow in spiritual gifts, although I really did not have a mature understanding of it at the time and I do not recall hearing any specific teachings about operating in spiritual gifts. The church continued to grow, and we were eventually forced to move into larger premises, but that's when I noticed things started to change. At first, I could not put my finger on it, but something was different in this new place. It began to feel like the focus was more on the church's image and high profile and it was at this new location where I was humiliatingly paraded about on the stage at our annual conference as mentioned earlier.

I thoroughly enjoyed singing in the church choir and became the leader of a men's house group that was very well attended. I was invited to speak on Christian television to tell my story about overcoming same-sex attractions by the leader of the organisation supporting Christians with unwanted same-sex attractions. This is something else I came to regret as I did not get to tell my story the way I would have preferred to, as the presenter seemed more interested in my past sexual encounter with a minister rather than where my life was currently. Then one day, God asked me a poignant question, *"Whose trophy, are you?"* I realised God was gently warning me about people's motives, and that I needed to be more discerning.

I was in this church for nine years before meeting the lady who would later become my wife. She was different from the other church girls, as this was not her first church experience. There was a maturity about her that I had not noticed in other women my own age in the church at that time. We dated secretly with the permission of the Senior Pastor for several months. Then in December 2000, we had a memorable public engagement in front of the whole church. Another revelation for me was the control being exerted by the church around our wedding plans. My fiancée had lost her mother a few months before, and the pain of not having her father at our wedding, who had passed away prematurely some years back, added some sadness to our wedding plans. She had always wanted to go to Hawaii since she was a little girl, and I suggested we should do the whole wedding there. Being somewhere different would make the ceremony a little easier to bear with her parents' absence. Only God knew that three months before the wedding, her brother would die unexpectedly, and her family would have a funeral to arrange before our wedding in August 2001.

My big mistake was sharing my plans in confidence with someone else, who immediately relayed it back to another couple who were doing the same thing. The man in question approached me angrily in church and said he was pleased that I was getting married but not happy about my choice to go to Hawaii and would be complaining to the pastor. I almost fell about laughing as I thought he was joking, until a few days later, I received a call to phone the church office. During that call to my pastor, I became aware of the reality of a controlling element in operation. I was told directly that this other couple had planned their wedding in Hawaii too, so I should reconsider our plans and marry in the UK instead. Furthermore, that I needed to remember there was a lot of competition in the church. My response was, *"I am not in competition; I am simply getting married"*. I was flabbergasted since I was fully expecting my pastor to encourage me to ignore the threats of the other groom in complaining about our plans as he was being immature.

As I thought about the phone call, I became furious and could not focus on my work once I returned to the office for the rest of the afternoon. *"Now, the church thinks it has a monopoly on Hawaii"*, I thought, and I started to question many things about the church from that day onwards. However, my fiancée and I stood our ground, as this was not a sin issue but a personal decision. So, we pressed on with our plans to marry in Hawaii and discovered that it was an extremely popular destination for thousands of people to get married from all over the world, especially from Japan. We had a wonderful time with a handful of our family in attendance for the first week in Honolulu, and after the wedding, we jetted off to visit the islands of Maui and Kauai for our three-week honeymoon. Looking back, I guess as he was my pastor and had been such great personal support to me, he merely wanted to officiate the ceremony himself.

From then onwards, the bitter disappointment with my church stayed hidden in my heart. Still, we agreed to a wedding blessing on our return the following month so family and friends in the UK could celebrate with us, and of course, my pastor officiated. Somehow, I could not get past the hurt

I still felt, and my enthusiasm for attending church took a steep nosedive, although I still went. One of the things I really had previously enjoyed about the church was our annual residential church conference, which was the highlight of the church's events calendar. It was a well-attended meeting with guest speakers flown in from America. I can honestly say God's presence was in those meetings, and I was always tremendously blessed, except for the time I was paraded across the stage to "testify". I usually always left there on a high and felt privileged to be part of the various teams, either in the mass choir, security, sound and filming crew, or part of the transportation crew. It was a big operation, and the buzz around it was electric.

However, one conference was noticeably different, and my wife and I wanted to return home after the very first night. I only stayed because I brought along my young teenage cousin, who was enjoying the fellowship with the other youth. We were not impressed with the conference at all, as we felt it resembled more of a motivational speaking event than a Christian church event. We felt oddly out of place and uncomfortable during the services, and it would be the last one we would attend.

Around this time, we had started attending prayer meetings during the week at a local church near to where I lived. We were hungry for more of what God had for us and felt we were not getting it in our current ministry. On two occasions, I had recently been to the hospital complaining of chest pains but was sent home with painkillers. A few days after the prayer meeting, I began coughing up coagulated blood. Whilst attending this prayer meeting, the minister praying for me said he felt led to lay hands on my chest, although he did not know why. If the blood clot had not come out of my mouth, I might not have realised the seriousness of my condition. However, despite this, the hospital still sent me home a third time, telling me to go and see my GP. I attended my GP surgery the next morning, and she was aghast that the hospital had sent me back home three times. She instructed me to return to the hospital with an accompanying letter, and they admitted me immediately and urgently injected warfarin into my stomach to thin down my blood. The next day, a scan confirmed that I had several blood clots on my lungs, and I was hospitalised for eight days, staying on blood-thinning medication for six months. If it were not for another leader's spiritual discernment, I might have died had the clot gone to my brain or affected my heart. Whilst in the hospital, I received a steady flow of visitors at all hours from my church. Not too long after this, my wife and I decided to visit another ministry further away from home at the invitation of a family member. Due to some health issues, we needed support with, I was informed that this new pastor was very gifted in helping people resolve issues like ours. Also, I was more than willing to receive any help being offered to me, but I had no clue what Satan was planning to do in order to destroy my marriage.

Out of the frying pan and into the fire

To say that my years in church so far had not prepared me for what would happen next is a colossal understatement. People were totally bamboozled by this leader's accurate "prophetic gift" in this new church setting. Consequently, my lack of discernment allowed me to become immersed in what I could only properly describe as a cult. Interestingly, one of the attractive things about this church was the sense of being part of a family, and the pastor often went out of his way to support and help many people financially and otherwise. People even from other ministries who had heard about his gifting would come to see him for "spiritual insight". I was unemployed for a time, so I accepted a full-time paid position as the church's office administrator. Initially, I felt really blessed but began noticing things that left me feeling uncomfortable. It was not long before he began to share with me what he claimed to be "seeing" about my future, including the presence of the spirit of death hanging around me.

He told me once of a vision he had where I suffered another blood clot and died on the operating table. Fear certainly gripped me, and I had absolutely no desire to die. Although I felt uncomfortable, in my naivety and gullibility, I followed his instructions and allowed him to lay hands on me and anoint me in highly inappropriate places. I would often be left feeling discouraged as he repeatedly claimed things were getting better spiritually, but then all of a sudden, they would come back with a vengeance, according to him. I felt like a yoyo, and it was not long before he crossed the line, even further claiming that God had told him to give me lots of time and attention, including travelling with him abroad for ministry purposes. I felt totally confused by his sexual advances toward me. My past life was behind me, and I had no desire to live that way again now that I had accepted Jesus Christ and I made it abundantly clear to him. Somehow, I managed to bury what was happening to me and function in other areas of my life as if things were perfectly normal, much like I had learned to as a child. Before long, other unemployed men were given positions in the office, and the church grew rapidly, and we had absolutely no clue as to the high level of spiritual bondage we were in.

This pastor was revered like a god, whilst at the same time abusing his power and authority to manipulate others and keeping them in perpetual bondage. There was an unspoken culture of silence even though many knew something was wrong because, after all, this was "an anointed man of God". Some left without saying goodbye, and others were left behind, wondering why they had disappeared so suddenly. He informed the office staff that others had rebelled against him, and God had removed them from the ministry. He would even almost braggingly relay stories of those who had come against him and had now been struck down with cancer. His verbally abusive and aggressive behaviour put fear in people and prevented the other leaders from successfully challenging him. He thought nothing of sharing confidential information about other people's private lives as a way of luring people into his so-called privileged inner circle. He was a master at making people feel "special", which caused many to let down their guard with him.

As I worked closely with him, and although I found it extremely difficult, I mustered up the courage to challenge him again privately about his behaviour, including his outbursts of extreme rage, amongst numerous other things. He could tell I was changing my attitude towards him and became warier in order to keep me on his side. The church came together and raised funds to buy him a brand-new Land Rover as a gift. He, in return, gave me his old car, which was now surplus to his requirements, and I agreed to give mine to another brother who needed a car. This was all part of the manipulation, although I was too blind to see it at the time. I prayed he would repent of his ways, and God told me I would be the one to expose him. I tried to dismiss the thought, asking God why He could not speak to him personally, but God was silent! Probably because God had spoken to him on many occasions, but he had refused to listen, and now, God's judgement was about to be executed. One day, during the middle of a worship service, I had what I would describe as an open vision. A giant hand came out from the wall behind the stage, grabbed hold of the pastor, and pulled him up and away out of his suit. The empty suit fell to the ground, and then I got onto the stage, pulled on the suit, and started to preach. The entire vision happened in a split second, and I was in a state of shock. I have never had an experience like it ever since.

Although I had firmly put my foot down and warned him off, I had no idea he was still sexually trying it on with other guys. I began to become suspicious about some of his private time in the office with others and although they were reluctant to speak at first, I felt led to keep pressing further. I soon discovered there were others he still had under his control and was manipulating due to their vulnerabilities. Stupidly, the thought never occurred to me that the problem was so widespread until another guy told me through tears about a recent sexual assault he had suffered in a hotel by this pastor. That was the beginning of the end. Another story soon emerged about his inappropriate behaviour, and along with two other guys, we decided to confront him privately. A very unwise thing to do, really, as we should have gone straight to the police. However, having emerged from a system where we were instructed to "touch not the Lord's anointed and do my prophets no harm", we struggled in our naivety to properly address the situation. We were gullible and clearly out of our depth. We did not realise how utterly broken and damaged we were, nor the high level of spiritual bondage and mass demonic oppression we were all under.

I began feeling as though I was having a nervous breakdown and sought Christian counselling outside the ministry before telling my wife everything. Though she was extremely hurt, she eventually appreciated how difficult and highly embarrassing it must have been to share things. Together, my wife and I immediately approached the rest of the leadership and set up a meeting. The other two witnesses attended and shared their stories. What became apparent over time is that my openness about my past struggles with same-sex attractions would be used against me. The focus was purposely shifted from the pastor to me, using my testimony as "proof" that I had been living a double life and was involved in a four-year "affair" with this leader. This was another lie that the enemy used to discredit me and damage my reputation. We later discovered that he had been targeting multitudes of unsuspecting males of all ages—married and single—of all shapes and sizes for many years. He had been doing this since his high school days back in his homeland, and one of his subordinate leaders who had known him since childhood confirmed this. Many had come to him vulnerable, needing to be healed of serious medical conditions or dealing with other pressing spiritual problems, but all that resulted was a trail of traumatised people and broken marriages due to his perverted behaviour and ungodly advice. Despite knowing all this and his track record, the leadership, including his own relative, continued supporting him as a senior leader.

The police contacted me as they had been approached by someone else who had given my name as someone to talk to. I divulged to the police what I had heard from witnesses, as they were eager to nail him once and for all. I gave a lengthy statement over two days to an officer who was part of the Sapphire Team: who specialised in crimes of sexual nature. They were absolutely convinced the Crown Prosecution Service would press charges now. I was encouraged to get as many people as possible to come forward with their stories to strengthen their case against him. I had been contacted by a family that had left after they heard we had been ejected from the church. They shared with us why they left and how they had discovered that the senior pastor had been previously arrested on four different occasions. On one occasion, it was for the lewd suggestions being made to young boys about taking their nude pictures, but formal charges were never made due to lack of evidence. Sadly, most of the other witnesses backed down either through fear and intimidation or were paid off to keep silent. Therefore, the Crown Prosecution Services was unable to press any charges despite the fact they had originally been extremely hopeful. Apparently, he had been on their radar for many years, being accused of sexually inappropriate behaviour towards minors. Still, he had always escaped prosecution due to insufficient evidence and a lack of credible witnesses. Before long, the church leadership, the congregation, and even those I considered friends, had been persuaded to turn against my wife and me. We were publicly accused of attempting to take over the church and destroy the senior pastor.

We were barred from the church premises, and I was suspended from my role in the church office on full pay until I was made redundant a few months later. The congregation, including a family member, was instructed to have nothing to do with us and cross the street to avoid us if they should see us. It became extremely nasty, with letters of death threats addressed to my wife and me. Some were even sent to my mother's home. We also received death threats by text from unknown numbers and were advised by the police to change our numbers, which we did. It was an excruciating and bitter time for us both. I took a few days away by myself to fast and pray about the situation. At the end of the fast, I felt led to pursue a claim against the church for sexual harassment and assault and an employment tribunal for constructive dismissal from my job in the church office. I had become a whistle-blower, and far from having my identity protected, which should have happened, the church made a scapegoat of me. During numerous church meetings, I was publicly berated and lied about from the pulpit in our absence.

I received a message from a guy I used to talk to but was close to the pastor. He wanted to meet in private, but I only agreed to meet in a public park somewhere. The day of the meeting came, but I kept getting a strong impression that I should not meet with him, so I cancelled our meeting. A few months later, I found out that the "pastor" had sent him to negotiate a large payoff for me to drop the case. My wife and I continued praying that the eyes of those still in the ministry would be opened. Eventually, through a series of events, another couple that had previously turned against us discovered the truth about the pastor and asked to meet with us to apologise to my wife and me for not believing us. They brought the guy to our house who was supposed to negotiate the payoff, as he had also discovered the truth about the pastor. He wanted to apologise personally to us and came to our home with the couple. He divulged much information, including a substantial payment promised to him by the pastor if he would make sure my wife and I and a few others were hospitalised to teach us a lesson.

Eventually, the church's insurance settled out of court, paying me compensation on my claims against the church for sexual harassment and sexual assault and fully reimbursed me for the cost to have counselling for several months due to the trauma I suffered. He also changed the church's name; hence, I could not pursue the employment claim, as they no longer legally existed. He was so angry that months later, he dared to bring a private lawsuit against me for thirty-four and half thousand pounds, claiming all sorts of nonsense about money and a car he allegedly loaned me. This was quite overwhelming for my wife and me, as we had no legal experience or training and had to defend the case ourselves.

God certainly has a great sense of humour as all the court paperwork and evidence we had prepared for the employment tribunal became the basis for our defence in his claim against us. One night, I had a dream where a judge in a courtroom gave me instructions to ask the claimant's solicitor certain questions. On waking, I jumped straight onto my computer whilst still in my pyjamas and wrote out the questions from my dream and emailed them to his solicitors. In court, almost eighteen months later, I defended myself and cross-examined him in the witness box to his utmost shame and humiliation, especially as he was supposed to have been a barrister before becoming a "pastor". My wife was with me, praying under her breath as she watched the proceedings. His behaviour on the stand was pathetic, and even his barrister that he brought in from Chancery Lane, London was embarrassed, whilst his solicitor hung his head in shame as I exposed his inconsistencies and questioned him as to why he was not allowed unsupervised contact with his own biological children. Something the judge pounced on immediately, drilling him as he tried to waffle his way out of giving a straight answer. The same questions God told me to ask in the dream are what the judge began to focus on during the trial. The judge severely challenged his solicitor for failing to respond adequately to questions I had put to them and providing evidence of their claim of which there was none. Following a four-hour hearing, the judge threw his ridiculous claims out, scolded him for being less than truthful, and made him repay all my legal fees in defending his claim against me. He was absolutely fuming and left the court that day with his tail firmly tucked between his legs. God granted us an amazing victory, one that I shall never forget, and it certainly increased my faith in God.

Life now

That was almost fourteen years ago, and life now is a very long way away from what it resembled back then. It was one of the most horrendous, soul-destroying, isolating, and lonely experiences that my wife and I have ever experienced. However, God absolutely used it to wake and shake us up from our slumber in religious "la la" land. Most importantly, God allowed the experience to cut us off from systems, ideologies, and people that were far from healthy and totally liberated us and our thinking about His Kingdom and His values. We learnt the importance of standing up for truth and exposing evil. We began mixing in different Christian circles and with diverse cultures. I began to experience God's love in a way I had not previously—meeting with and being mentored and trained by seasoned, spiritually mature believers who God was using. They displayed His deep love for us and compassion. I began my journey of deep inner healing and was delivered from a host of demonic entities. Evil spirits that had attached themselves to me even before becoming a believer now had no more legal rights in my life. I was also delivered from demons that had come into my life whilst I had submitted myself to ungodly leadership. It was quite overwhelming at times to realise the level of demonic oppression I was under and the amount of damage my spirit had experienced between the times of my abusive childhood and my deliverance from the ungodly situations mentioned above. Still, God lovingly peeled back the layers bit by bit and opened my eyes. His deep Fatherly love enabled me to have compassion towards myself when I realised that my unhealed wounds that had never been addressed in my early Christian walk, had left me vulnerable to further wounding and demonic oppression later on. I am not trying to blame anyone, just simply stating a profound spiritual truth. It has also given me a healthy respect and a greater scriptural understanding of the spiritual warfare the Church faces during these end times.

I have experienced a catalogue of other Church hurts over the years, many of which I have not mentioned for brevity's sake, between my chorister days at age eleven, right up until being kicked out of the church and having former friends turn against us. I am not faultless either, and no doubt, I have also made mistakes, made wrong decisions during my journey, and have hurt others too. I have simply asked God for His forgiveness and healing for those I have wronged in any way. Although it was a painful and humiliating experience, God used it to prepare me for what He had planned for us all along. Despite all the negatives, it was whilst in those churches, that I began developing leadership skills. I practised teaching, preaching, and visiting other ministries that were not Pentecostal or believed only they had "the truth". I learned how to stand up and confront corrupt leaders and their demonic systems. I learnt that just because people "act" like friends, I need to be more discerning and not so gullible. I learned to go against the tide of those jumping on the bandwagon of popularity and follow God's leading instead. I learned that God is my Father, spiritual covering, advisor, comforter, counsellor, and best friend. I also see that no matter how broken your life may be, how many mistakes you make, or how much others may have written you off, God simply needs a heart towards Him and a willingness to humbly be used by Him. Furthermore, during our healing journey, God allowed us to start socialising with Christians from a wider range of cultures and denominations than we had previously been exposed to. He challenged our thinking and enabled us to see him working in places beyond denominational constraints, and we experienced significant healing and growth spiritually and emotionally.

God has brought my wife and me a long way and has strengthened and matured us tremendously through the process. I learned many things along the way, which helped shape my character into what I am today as a husband and pastor with the privilege of looking after God's people. A verse that really resonates with me is: *And we know [with great confidence] that God [who is deeply concerned about us] causes all things to work together [as a plan] for good for those who love God, to those who are called according to His plan and purpose* (**Romans 8:28**; AMP).

Because of my relationship with God, I have realised my bright future is not based on past mistakes, others' views, or erroneous judgments about me. I am what God has called me to be and can do whatever He alone has called me to do. I do not hold any malice or ill will towards those that have misused, abused, ill-treated, belittled, rejected, and hurt us in various ways, shapes, or forms. I simply see it as the brokenness of mankind and the evil work of Satan using people's weaknesses for his agenda. One of the most important things I have learned is that forgiveness is a beautiful, powerful, and healing tool God gave to overcome past hurts and sincerely let go of things highly detrimental to our mental, emotional, and spiritual well-being. As a result, I have developed far more compassion for others that have been hurt and wounded, and most importantly, developed a far greater perspective of God and His purposes.

It still saddens me that so many people are still stuck in abusive churches and struggling to find their way out. Or they have left their group but are no longer fellowshipping with anybody in the Body of Christ. Perhaps they are not even aware of the dangers of the situation they are in. These are the unfortunate realities of what can happen if we do not have a biblical understanding of what the Church should look like, how leaders should be operating and our authority as joint heirs with Jesus Christ. As a result, we are more vulnerable to the dictates and shenanigans of charlatans dressed in sheep's clothing. My passion for people being free from abusive church situations and healing from inflicted wounds on them comes from my own journey and I count it an absolute privilege to use my experiences to help others in any way possible. There is great hope after church hurt and spiritual abuse, and absolutely nothing is too hard for God. Amen!

Bibliography

Bell, A. P. *Breaking the Chains of Mental Slavery*, A & M Publishing, April Cottage, Ellis Avenue, Chalfont Heights, Chalfont St Peter, Gerrards Cross, Bucks, SL9 9AU, England, U.K. 2013.

Chrnalogar, M. A. *Twisted Scriptures*, Zondervan, Grand Rapids, Michigan, 49530, U.S.A. 2000.

Colson, C. with Ellen Santilli Vaughn, *The Body, being light in the darkness*, World Publishing, USA, 1992.

Johnson, D & Van Vonderen, J. *The Subtle Power of Spiritual Abuse*, Bethany House Publishers, 11400 Hampshire Avenue South, Bloomington, Minnesota 5548, U.S.A. 1991.

Prince, D. *They Shall Expel Demons*, Derek Prince Ministries-UK.1998.

Williams, T.D. (Dr). *The Bible is Black History*, Self-Publishing Services: WritersTablet.org, 2018.

Webpages

Adults Abused by Clergy, www.adultsabusedbyclergy.org, [10th June 2022]

About the Author

Colin became a born-again Christian in June 1992. Over the years whilst working through his own issues which resulted from a traumatic and abusive childhood, he became increasingly aware that God was calling him to help others that had been hurt and wounded in ways both alike and dissimilar to his own. Due to his openness about his own battles, he was invited to speak at various Christian conferences in the U.K and abroad and was privileged to share his testimony on Christian television.

He soon found himself being asked to lead support groups for men and taught seminars at Men's conferences in the U.K on issues pertaining to the dangers of pornography and sexual addiction. Appreciating the enormity of his calling, he obtained a post graduate diploma in counselling at Goldsmiths, University of London, whilst simultaneously practicing as a voluntary counsellor for One in Four; an organisation based in Southeast London, specialising in working with adult survivors of sexual abuse. He obtained his BTh (Hons) Ministerial Theology at Roehampton University, London.

Though there have been many challenges, Colin became more determined to expose unethical practices in the church and fulfil his God ordained purpose. His calling as a Pastor was confirmed by other seasoned Christian leaders and in

January 2010 he was officially ordained. Colin and his wife Yvonne jointly preside over Love House Fellowship and relocated from London to Lincolnshire, U.K. in January 2020.

Other resources & contact details

Colin & Yvonne minister together as a couple and are happy to consider attending your event as guest speakers.

They also run seminars & workshops on

- When Church Hurts
- Deliverance & Healing
- Moving from trauma to triumph
- Overcoming Sexual addictions
- And other topics

They are available for personal ministry appointments via zoom.

Please contact them for information about ways that they can help and for dates of upcoming events.

email: masoncol@gmail.com

CPSIA information can be obtained
at www.ICGtesting.com
Printed in the USA
BVHW092340290123
657302BV00015B/2309